MEALS·MICROWAVE STYLE

MENUS
&
RECIPES

D1802513

ELLIE TOPP • BETTY SHIELDS

GAI-GARET

Published by
Gai-Garet Design & Publication Ltd.
Carp, Ontario, Canada K0A 1L0
(613) 839-2915

ISBN 0-921165-05-6
Printed and bound in Canada
©1988 by Ellie Topp and Betty Shields

Photography by Garry Carter
　　　　　　　Garry Carter Photography Limited
　　　　　　　Ottawa, Ontario
Nutritional Analysis by A.D. Harvey Nutrition Consultants
　　　　　　　Ottawa, Ontario
Designed by Wendelina O'Keefe
Food Styling by Wendelina O'Keefe
Editor: Gail Pike
　　　　Gai-Garet Design & Publication Ltd.
　　　　Carp, Ontario

Canadian Cataloguing in Publication Data

Topp, Ellie, 1938–
　　Meals microwave style: menus and recipes

Includes index.
ISBN 0-921165-05-6

1. Microwave cookery.　2. Menus.　I. Shields, Betty　II. Title.

TX832.T66 1988　641.5'882　C88-090329-5

Cover Menu:

Poulet Chasseur (p. 80)
Green Fettucine (p. 125)
Rosemary Carrots (p. 105)

Foreword

For years microwave ovens and Betty's Kitchen have been synonymous in the Ottawa area. Countless numbers of Ottawans learned the ABCs of microwave in the cooking schools attached to the Betty's Kitchen shops. It was just a matter of time before a microwave cookbook was written by Betty Shields and her associates.

Ellie Topp, the director of the three cooking schools, is the main driving force behind this book, and it's obvious that she has been listening to what her students have said they want and need to know. This is not just another recipe book. Ellie has organized her material in a way most useful to today's busy consumer. Recipes are organized into interesting menus, with time charts and grocery lists provided. This will be a valuable help for people wishing to learn to make better use of their planning, shopping and cooking time.

As you would expect from a cooking teacher, there are lots of helpful little hints, gathered over the years, and probably recognized by Ellie's former students. Nutritional analysis of each recipe is especially welcome to those concerned about healthy eating.

The mystery of microwave cooking is diminishing and people are becoming more comfortable using their ovens. The majority of kitchens now contain at least one microwave, and the numbers are constantly increasing. We should all be encouraged to use our microwaves for more than reheating coffee!

I congratulate Ellie Topp, Betty Shields and Gail Pike on the publication of this "user-friendly" cookbook. It will do its part to promote more intelligent microwave use.

Pam Collacott
Owner, Trillium Cooking School
Ottawa Citizen Food Writer

NOTES FROM THE AUTHORS

This book exists because we have been involved in teaching microwave cooking, microwave recipe development and microwave sales for over a decade. For several years many of our friends and clients have urged us to compile a microwave cookbook. In the fall of 1987 we compiled our first microwave cookbook *Capital Cooks* as a fund raising project for the Ottawa Food Bank. Our goal for this book is to provide you with the skills to make your microwave meal preparation efficient, nutritious and above all delicious.

The authors would like to thank all the staff of Betty's Kitchen who helped with the recipe testing and gave their comments and suggestions. Thanks also to Pam Collacott, Food Writer — Ottawa Citizen, for the use of one recipe and Danielle Latremouille, owner of Chanterelle Catering, for use of two recipes.

Table of Contents

Helpful Information For Great Microwave Cooking

POWER LEVELS

Power level designations differ with different brands of ovens. These recipes were tested in 700 watt ovens with the following levels relating to percentage of 700 watts. If your oven is other than 700 watts, read your manufacturer's information for the appropriate wattage. In general you will need to add about 25% more time for a 500 watt oven and 15% for a 600 oven.

HIGH	100%	700 watts (approximate)
MEDIUM	70%	490 watts (approximate)
MEDIUM-LOW	50%	360 watts (approximate)
LOW	30%	200 watts (approximate)
WARM	10%	70 watts (approximate)

COOKING TIMES

Cooking time is a critical factor in obtaining good results in microwave cooking. The length of time depends on the **quantity of food**, as well as the **wattage used** and the **density of the food**. The table below has been compiled for commonly cooked foods. For accurate timing weigh food before cooking (subtracting the weight of the dish) and estimate the cooking time by multiplying the weight by the minutes per kilogram or pound.

Meat and Poultry

Meat and poultry should be fully defrosted and at refrigerator temperature. Allow 12 minutes per pound of food for defrosting time in ovens with a defrost program. To cook roasts or poultry, place on a microwavable rack and insert a microwave meat thermometer or probe. Cover with parchment or wax paper and cook to temperature indicated estimating time according to weight per kilogram or pound. Allow 15-20 minutes of standing time, covered, to complete cooking for roasts; 5 minutes for chicken pieces. During this time the temperature will rise 10°F.

	POWER LEVEL	TIME/ KG / POUND	TEMP
Poultry			
Chicken pieces	MEDIUM (70%)	18 min./ 8 min.	
Boneless turkey breast	MEDIUM (70%)	22 min./10 min.	170°F
Chicken & Turkey — whole	MEDIUM (70%)	22 min./10 min.	170°F
Beef			
Tender roasts (rib, loin)			
Rare	MEDIUM (70%)	18-22 min./ 8-10 min.	125°F
Medium	MEDIUM (70%)	22-26 min./10-12 min.	135°F
Well	MEDIUM (70%)	26-30 min./12-14 min.	155°F

Tougher roasts
  Chuck, pot,
  cross rib

Place in enough liquid to cover halfway. Bring to a boil on HIGH (100%) power, then cook on LOW (30%) for 60-90 minutes. Turn over halfway during cooking time.

Pork			
loin	MEDIUM (70%)	30-35 min./14-16 min.	170°F
shoulder	MED-LOW (50%)	33-41 min./15-19 min.	170°F
Ham cooked, boneless	MED-LOW (50%)	22-26 min./10-12 min.	130°F
bone	MED-LOW (50%)	22-26 min./10-12 min.	130°F
Lamb	MED-LOW (50%)	24-28 min./11-13 min.	160°F
Fish			
Covered loosely*	HIGH (100%)	13 min./6 min.	
Covered tightly**	HIGH (100%)	11 min./5 min.	

VEGETABLES — rinse in cold water and shake. Cover tightly.

Broccoli, cauliflower	HIGH (100%)	13 min./6 min.	
Green Beans***	HIGH (100%)	13 min./6 min.	
Carrots***, potatoes	HIGH (100%)	18 min./8 min.	
Asparagus, zucchini	HIGH (100%)	9 min./4 min.	

* Covered loosely means with parchment or wax paper.

** Covered tightly means with a tightfitting casserole lid or plastic wrap

*** Soak in cold water for 5-15 minutes before cooking. Drain and add 25 mL (2 Tbsp.) water to cooking container.

Microwave Techniques

1. Covering foods — In microwave cooking heat is generated in the foods only and not in the oven. Therefore covering retains the steam and heat in the food which gives faster and more even cooking. This is especially evident with low heat conducting utensils such as thermoplastic. Use a tight cover such as a lid or plastic wrap for foods which are moist (vegetables, casseroles). Use a partial cover such as wax or parchment paper which allows some steam to escape while holding

the heat close to the food where browning and crisping is desired (meats and baking).

2. Stirring — Food cooked by microwave energy cooks first on the outside. If you stir you move the hot outside to the center giving more even cooking. For foods which cannot be stirred such as large roasts, turn over or rearrange pieces once or twice during cooking.

3. Arranging — How food is arranged for microwave cooking is very important. If you arrange foods with the most dense part to the out-side rearranging is not necessary. Chicken legs cook well putting the large part of the leg to the outside. This technique also allows you to cook a vegetable platter of vegetables with different cooking times by arranging the longest cooking vegetables on the outside (broccoli or cauliflower) and a short cooking vegetable (zucchini) in the centre.

4. Shielding — Small pieces of foil are used where it is desirable to stop overcooking by reflecting energy away from that area. For example shield legs and wings of a chicken and the corners of a square pan. To prevent arcing of foil in the microwave it is important that the foil be smooth and be no closer that 2.5 cm (1 inch) to the sides of the oven. The foil should never cover more than $1/3$ to $1/2$ of the food area.

Microwavable Cookware

The material, shape and size of microwavable cookware affects the time required to cook food in the microwave, as well as the evenness of cooking. What you cook IN affects what you get OUT.

Although you will have some suitable dishes in your cupboard to start with such as heat resistant glass, ceramic and clay pots, you will eventually want to expand your cookware selection for the microwave's specific requirements. For best results select compact multipurpose pieces in low heat conducting materials. Look for clear pans for good visibility, raised bottoms and vents allowing steam to escape, lids and handles for convenience.

Suitable Materials
   Thermoplastics — utensils low in heat transfer. (Poor conductors insure maximum quality.)
      Thermoplastics
      a) allow foods to retain heat longer
      b) allow more even heating and faster cooking
      c) allow better browning
      d) minimize the need to stir, turn or shield to prevent overcooking

(Note: Only plastic marked suitable for microwave use should be used in a microwave oven.)

Heat resistant glass, Corning Ware, thermoset plastics

Shapes
Round or donut shapes provide more even results as the reflected energy from the oven walls bounces back and forth in a criss-cross pattern. Rectangular or square shapes result in a cross over of energy on corners that can cause uneven cooking or overcooking unless corners are shielded. Donut shapes allow energy to penetrate from both the outside and center to speed the cooking process by about 20%.

Size of Utensils
For best results, choose a dish close in size to the amount of food being cooked. Foods low in moisture cook best in cookware with low sides ie. a 2 L (2 qt.) cake pan or tray. High moisture foods cook best in cylindrical shapes ie. pots with higher sides than diameter. For foods such as rice and cereal a container that holds twice the volume of food and liquid combined is needed to accommodate a full boil.

Microwavable Cookware Allowing For Full Use of This Book
a) Ring/tube pans — 1.5 L and 3 L (6 cup and 12 cup) with straight flexible sides to eliminate greasing
b) Roasting rack — multiple purpose racks are available which allow grease to drip away from meat. Also doubles as a bacon rack and as a trivet for elevating cakes
c) 2 L (2 qt.) cake/casserole pan with 6 to 7.5 cm (2 1/2 to 3 inch) flexible sides for larger volume in microwave cakes
d) High-sided cylindrical shaped 3 L (3 qt.) pot with tight lid for simmering foods or milk and pasta products requiring slow cooking or larger volume
e) Muffin pans — thermoplastic with vents for elimination of moisture/condensation
f) Browning dishes — special cookware designed to be heated before use. These dishes give a nicely browned product and are excellent for cooking thin meats such as steaks or chicken rolls. Browning dishes with lids can be used for continued cooking of tougher meats such as Swiss steak or stews.

RECIPE CALLS FOR:	MICRO MAC UTENSILS TO USE
1. 3L/3qt.	MM-04 MICRO SIMMER POT
2. 1-2L/1-2qt. covered veg.	MM-035 MINI ROAST &
	BAKE SET
3. 2L/2qt. or 8-9″ PAN	MM-30 CAKE'N'COOK PAN
or 1L/1qt.	(part of MM-035 set)
4. 750mL/3cup or	MM-44 PETIT TOTE POT
500 mL/2cup or	
small microwavable container	
5. 1.5L/6 cup	MM-21 RING MOLD
6. 2.5L/2½qt or	MM-07 REVERSA MICROTRAY
18cm × 28cm/7″ × 11″	(bottom of PairO'Trays)
7. 3L/12cup thermoplastic	MM-06 FLUTED TUBE
tube pan	
8. MUFFIN PAN	MM-10 MINICAKER
9. MICROWAVABLE RACK	MM-09 MULTI RAX

NOTE: MM-88 MINI STEAM'N'POACH SET PROVIDES YOU WITH
NO. 2;3;5;8; plus 7 MINICUPS & recipe book.

Hints For Efficient Meal Preparation

For today's families the time between arriving home and dinner is all too short for a hungry family anticipating the evening meal. In order to make pre-dinner preparation as quick as possible, we have made suggestions that may help you prepare a good nutritious dinner in 30 to 45 minutes.

1. Defrost meat in the microwave early in the day according to your oven's defrost program. Store in the refrigerator until time to prepare the meal or overnight.

2. Dessert and often parts of other dishes can be prepared the night before. This will shorten the preparation time considerably before the meal is served. Generally this does not sacrifice quality as dessert is often best served chilled, and long cooking items such as rice or stews can be quickly reheated without loss of flavour.

3. Generally prepare and cook the dish with the longest cooking time first since it will usually have the longest standing time. Then, while the first one is cooking prepare the second dish to be cooked so that it is ready to go in the oven when the first dish is finished.

4. When preparing whole meals in your microwave, use microwavable cookware with close fitting covers to help foods stay hot while others are cooking. Plan to undercook the first food cooked, as a longer standing time will finish cooking it. This will prevent overcooking during standing time or reheating.

THE MENU APPROACH

The Menu Approach

Introduction

Even with the speed of microwave cooking, to be truly efficient organization is required to minimize the time needed for shopping and food preparation. This section shows you a way to organize your family meal preparation time by providing a weekly menu plan and shopping list for three different weeks. Once you are familiar with this approach and the time it saves, you can easily plan your own weekly menus and shopping plan. No longer will "Are we having that again?" be heard around your kitchen.

Note: Plan dinner menus for the week following Canada's Food Guide. Adjust recipes if you are cooking for other than 4 people or if you wish to freeze extra portions for easy meals later.

Canada's Food Guide

milk and milk products
Children up to
11 years 2–3 servings
Adolescents 3–4 servings
Pregnant and nursing
women 3–4 servings
Adults 2 servings

meat, fish poultry and alternates
2 servings

breads and cereals
3–5 servings
whole grain or
enriched

fruits and vegetables
4–5 servings
Include at least
two vegetables

A dinner menu plan follows that is designed to serve 4 people for 3 weeks. Each week has 6 menus, leaving the 7th day free for eating out or making use of "planned-overs". The entree, vegetables and dessert have been included. Of course, you may wish to add the accompaniments such as salads and rolls, or choose an appetizer from those included in the recipe section. A shopping list follows the family menu suggestions. It has been prepared for each week and organized according to food groups corresponding to grocery store sections, making shopping as efficient as possible.

The times indicated in the following menus are the times generally required by the authors to prepare the dishes listed. A food processor was used extensively and the kitchen was well equipped with cookware and utensils to allow efficient preparation. The time is, therefore, only a rough guide depending on the speed of work, the equipment available and, of course, a minimum of interruptions. <u>Preparing</u> includes anything that can be done before cooking ie. peeling vegetables, measuring and mixing ingredients etc. <u>Cooking</u> refers to the actual cooking time in the microwave oven.

Week 1

Golden Glazed Chicken (p. 79)
Browned Potato Wedges (p. 121)
Brussels Sprouts and Water Chestnuts (p. 104)
Chocolate Upside Down Cake (p. 155)

PLAN OF ACTION:
The night before serving time:
 1. Prepare and cook Chocolate Upside Down Cake
Approximately 45 minutes before serving time:
 1. Prepare and cook Golden Glazed Chicken. While chicken is cooking prepare Potato Wedges.
 2. Cook Potato Wedges through step 1. While potatoes are cooking prepare Brussels Sprouts and Water Chestnuts.
 3. Cook Brussels Sprouts.
 4. Finish cooking potatoes.

Tuna with Green Beans and Rice (p. 91)
Apple Crisp (p. 142)

PLAN OF ACTION:
45 minutes before or the night before serving time:
 1. Cook 125 mL (1/2 cup) rice with 250 mL(1 cup) water and 2 mL (1/2 tsp.) salt unless you have some leftover rice on hand. Cover and store in refrigerator if preparing the night before.
Approximately 25 minutes before serving time:
 1. Prepare and cook Tuna with Green Beans and Rice. While casserole is cooking prepare Apple Crisp.
 2. Cook Crisp while eating dinner. Serve warm with ice cream or whipped cream.

Herbed Lamb Chops with Vegetables (p. 68)
Florida Key Lime Pie (p. 138)

PLAN OF ACTION:
The night before serving time:
 1. Prepare and cook Key Lime Pie. Chill until serving time.
Approximately 45 minutes before serving time:
 1. Prepare and cook Herbed Lamb Chops with Vegetables.

Veal Cordon Bleu (p. 67)
Wild Rice and Vegetables (p. 118)
Orange Cream Dessert (p. 129)

PLAN OF ACTION:
One hour or the night before serving time:
> 1. Prepare and cook Orange Cream Dessert.
> 2. Prepare and cook Wild Rice and Vegetables through step 2, cooking for 12 minutes instead of 15. Cover and place in refrigerator if preparing the night before.

Approximately 30 minutes before serving time:
> 1. Micro-cook rice on HIGH (100%) for 4 minutes or until hot.
> 2. Meanwhile prepare vegetables for rice. When rice is hot cook vegetables as in step 3. Keep warm.
> 3. Prepare and cook Veal Cordon Bleu.

Poulet Chasseur (p. 80)
Green Fettuccine (p. 125)
Rosemary Carrots (p. 105)
Caribbean Bananas (p. 144)

PLAN OF ACTION:
45 minutes or the night before serving time:
> 1. Prepare and cook Poulet Chasseur. Cover and store in refrigerator if preparing the night before.

Approximately 25 minutes before serving time:
> 1. If prepared the night before reheat chicken on MEDIUM (70%) approximately 6 to 8 minutes or until heated through. Keep warm. While chicken is heating peel and soak carrots.
> 2. Cook Rosemary Carrots.
> 3. Prepare Green Fettuccine (may be cooked conventionally if desired while chicken is heating). While fettuccine is cooking prepare Caribbean Bananas.
> 4. After dinner cook bananas.

Sweet and Sour Meatballs (p. 59)
Rice
Glazed Squash (p. 114)
Brownies and Ice Cream (p. 172)

PLAN OF ACTION:
One hour or the night before serving time:
    1. Prepare and cook Brownies.
    2. Prepare and cook Sweet and Sour Sauce Sauce.
    3. Prepare and cook rice: In a 3 L (3 qt.) container combine 250 mL (1 cup) rice with 500 mL (2 cups) hot water and 5 mL (1 tsp.) salt. Micro-cook on HIGH (100%) for 5 minutes or until boiling and then on LOW (30%) for 10 minutes. Cover and store in refrigerator if preparing the night before.
Approximately 30 minutes before serving time:
    1. Cook Glazed Squash and keep warm. While squash is cooking prepare Sweet and Sour Meatballs.
    2. Cook meatballs.
    3. If prepared the night before reheat rice on HIGH for 4 minutes or until heated through. Stir parsley into rice.

Week 2

Fish Rings Florentine (p. 87)
Carrots and Snow Peas (p. 106)
Potato Puff (p. 120)
Oatmeal Spice Cake with Coconut Pecan Topping (p. 154)

PLAN OF ACTION:
One hour or the night before serving time:
    1. Prepare and cook Oatmeal Spice Cake with Coconut Pecan Topping.
    2. The night before place fish in refrigerator to defrost or one hour before defrost fish on defrost program and keep in refrigerator.
Approximately 40 minutes before serving time:
    1. Prepare and cook Potato Puff and keep warm. While potatoes cook peel carrots and set aside to soak. Prepare Fish Rings Florentine.
    2. Cook fish. While fish cooks prepare Carrots and Snow Peas.
    3. Cook Carrots and Snow Peas.

Beef Vegetable Stir-Fry (p. 53)
Rice
Almond Float (p. 146)

PLAN OF ACTION:
The night before serving time:
     1. Prepare Almond Float
Approximately 40 minutes before serving time:
     1. Prepare and cook rice: Combine 250 mL (1 cup) rice,
     500 mL (2 cups) hot water and 5 mL (1 tsp.) salt in a
     3 L (3 qt.) microwave container. Micro-cook on HIGH
     (100%) for 5 minutes or until boiling, and then on LOW
     (30%) for 10 minutes. While rice is cooking prepare
     vegetables for Beef Vegetable Stir Fry. Let rice stand while
     cooking beef.
     2. Cook beef stir-fry. While beef is cooking prepare Almond
     Float for serving.

Herbed Chicken Breasts and Peas with Rice (p. 75)
Gingerbread with Orange Cream Cheese Topping (p. 158)

PLAN OF ACTION:
Approximately 45 minutes before serving time:
     1. Cook rice in step 1 of Herbed Chicken Breasts and Peas
     with Rice. While rice is cooking prepare Gingerbread with
     Orange Cream Sauce.
     2. Cook gingerbread. While gingerbread is cooking prepare
     ingredients for chicken.
     3. Cook chicken breasts. While chicken is cooking prepare
     sauce for gingerbread.

Savory Pork Ragout (p. 65)
Parsley Potatoes (p. 122)
Broccoli and Cheese Sauce (p. 102)
Fresh Fruit Meringues (p. 140)

PLAN OF ACTION:
One hour or the night before serving time:

> 1. Prepare and cook Savory Pork Ragout. Cover and store in refrigerator if preparing the night before.

Approximately 30 minutes before serving time:

> 1. If prepared the night before heat ragout on MEDIUM for 4-6 minutes stirring twice until hot. Keep warm. Meanwhile prepare Parsley Potatoes.
> 2. Cook potatoes. While potatoes cook prepare Fresh Fruit Meringues.
> 3. Cook meringues.
> 4. Prepare and cook broccoli: rinse broccoli and arrange on a flat microwave serving dish arranging spears in a ring with heads pointing out. Cover with plastic wrap or lid and micro-cook on HIGH (100%) for 13 minutes per kg or 8 minutes per pound. While broccoli is cooking prepare cheese sauce.
> 5. Cook cheese sauce.

Salmon and Pasta with Vegetables (p. 85)
Kahlua Pie (p. 137)

PLAN OF ACTION:
The night before serving time:

> 1. Prepare and cook Kahlua Pie. Chill until serving time.

Approximately 30 minutes before serving time:

> 1. Prepare and cook Salmon and Pasta with Vegetables

Savory Meatloaf (p. 58)
Cheese Potatoes (p. 122)
Harvard Beets (p. 101)
Carrot Cake with Cream Cheese Glaze (p. 162)

PLAN OF ACTION:
The night before serving time:

> 1. Prepare and cook one half recipe Carrot Cake with Cream Cheese Glaze.

Approximately 40 minutes before serving time:

> 1. Prepare and cook Savory Meatloaf. While meatloaf is cooking prepare Cheese Potatoes.
> 2. Cook potatoes. While potatoes are cooking prepare Harvard Beets.
> 3. Cook beets.

Week 3

Chicken Rolls with Two Cheeses (p. 72)
Potato and Green Pepper Ratatouille (p. 123)
Apple Ginger Upside Down Cake (p. 156)

PLAN OF ACTION:
One hour or the night before serving time:
   1. Prepare and cook Apple Ginger Upside Down Cake.
Approximately 40 minutes before serving time:
   1. Prepare Chicken Rolls with Two Cheeses.
   2. Prepare and cook Potato and Green Pepper Ratatouille.
   3. Cook chicken rolls.

Beef Stroganoff with Noodles (p. 51)
Green Beans with Prosciutto (p. 109)
Cherries Jubilee (p. 145)

PLAN OF ACTION:
Approximately 40 minutes before serving time:
   1. Cook noodles (8 oz. or 250 g uncooked) or plan to cook
   on conventional stove while stroganoff is cooking. Drain and
   rinse in hot water. Toss with 15 mL (1 Tbsp.) butter to coat.
   2. Prepare and cook Beef Stroganoff. While stroganoff is
   cooking prepare Green Beans with Prosciutto.
   3. Cook beans and reheat noodles if necessary
   4. While beans are cooking prepare Cherries Jubilee.
   5. After dinner cook Cherries Jubilee.

Salmon Cups with Parsley Sauce (p. 86)
Peas and Mushrooms (p. 110)
Confetti Rice (p. 117)
Pineapple Squares (p. 169)

PLAN OF ACTION:
The night before serving time:
    1. Prepare and cook Pineapple Squares.
Approximately 30 minutes before serving time:
    1. Prepare and cook Confetti Rice. Meanwhile prepare
Salmon Cups.
    2. Cook salmon cups. Prepare sauce while salmon is cooking.
    3. Prepare and cook Peas and Mushrooms.
    4. Cook sauce for salmon. Turn out salmon cups and pour
sauce over.

Marmalade Ham (p. 65)
Mushroom Spinach Bake (p. 113)
Soufflé Potatoes (p. 120)
Floating Islands (p. 133)

PLAN OF ACTION:
One hour or the night before serving time:
    1. Prepare and cook Floating Islands.
Approximately 30 minutes before serving time:
    1. Prepare and cook potatoes for Soufflé Potatoes. While
potatoes are cooking prepare Mushroom Spinach Bake.
    2. Prepare and cook Marmalade Ham. While ham is cooking
finish potatoes.
    3. Cook spinach.

Quick Beef-Zucchini Casserole (p. 61)
Rum and Raisin Bread Pudding with Custard Sauce (p. 149)

PLAN OF ACTION:
One hour or the night before serving time:
> 1. Prepare and cook Rum and Raisin Pudding. If keeping overnight cover and chill in refrigerator.

Approximately 40 minutes before serving time:
> 1. Prepare and cook Beef-Zucchini Casserole. While casserole is cooking prepare Custard Sauce.
> 2. Cook custard sauce. Let cool.
> 3. Reheat pudding slightly if desired. It may be served warm or cold.

Crusty Fried Chicken (p. 79)
Horseradish Potatoes and Cream (p. 123)
Broccoli with Sesame Seed Butter (p. 102)
Fresh Fruit with Grand Marnier Sauce (p. 191)

PLAN OF ACTION:
One hour or the night before serving time:
> 1. Prepare and cook Horseradish Potatoes and Cream. Cover and store in refrigerator if preparing the night before.

Approximately 40 minutes before serving time:
> 1. If prepared the night before reheat potatoes on HIGH (100%) for 4 minutes or until hot. Keep warm on warming tray or in warm place. While potatoes are heating prepare Crusty Chicken.
> 2. Cook chicken. While chicken is cooking prepare Broccoli with Sesame Seed Butter and prepare fresh fruit.
> 3. Cook broccoli. While broccoli is cooking prepare Grand Marnier Sauce.
> 4. Cook sauce.

SHOPPING LIST

Remember to * add foods required for breakfast, lunch and snacks
* add any household or personal items needed
* check staple list for any items that need replenishing

WEEK 1

Canned Goods

1 small can water chestnuts
1 can 284 mL or 10 oz. cream of
  mushroom soup
1 can (182 mL or 6.5 oz.) tuna
1 can (300 mL or 11 oz.)
  sweetened condensed milk
1 can mandarin oranges
1 small can tomato sauce
1 small can tomato paste
1 can (540 mL or 19 oz.)
  pineapple tidbits

Meat and Poultry

4 pieces chicken (legs and thighs or
  2 whole breasts)
4 shoulder lamb chops (500 g or
  1 lb. total weight)
4 pieces veal fillet
4 thin slices ham
1 frying chicken
500 g or 1 lb. lean ground beef

Fresh Fruits and Vegetables

4 medium potatoes
1 bunch parsley
6-8 cooking apples
1.5 kg or 3 lb. carrots
150 g or 5 oz. fresh green beans
500 g or 1 lb. small new potatoes
375 g or 12 oz. fresh mushrooms
5-6 limes
2 lemons
3 dry shallots
1 small green pepper
1 kg or 2 lb. pepper squash
2 large bananas

Dairy Products

1 doz. eggs
250 mL or 1 cup milk
125 g or 4 oz. cream cheese
125 mL or ½ cup whipping cream
75 mL or ⅓ cup half and half or
  cereal cream
50 mL or ¼ cup cottage cheese
900 g or 2 lb. butter
125 g or 4 oz. Parmesan cheese
60 g or 2 oz. Edam cheese
30 g or 1 oz. Swiss cheese

Frozen Foods

500 g or 1 lb. Brussels sprouts
300 g or 12 oz. French-style green
  beans
1 small can orange juice
500 mL or 1 pint vanilla ice cream

Miscellaneous

45 mL or ¼ cup Dijon mustard
175 mL or ¾ cup flaked coconut
125 mL or ½ cup granola
75 mL or ⅓ cup oatmeal
300 mL or 1 ¼ cup graham
  crumbs
2 pkgs unflavoured gelatin
75 mL or ⅓ cup wild rice
125 mL or ½ cup dry bread
  crumbs
50 mL or ¼ cup honey
25 mL or 2 Tbsp. cider vinegar
375 g or 12 oz. green fettuccini
15 mL or 1 Tbsp. soy sauce

Wine or Liquor

250 mL or 1 cup white wine
40 mL or ¼ cup orange liqueur
15 mL or 1 Tbsp. brandy
25 mL or 2 Tbsp. dark rum

WEEK 2

Canned Goods

1 can mandarin oranges
1 can (540 mL or 19 oz.) tomatoes
1 small can pears
1 small can peaches
2 cans (213 g or 7.5 oz.) salmon
1 can (540 mL or 19 oz.) beets
250 g or 10 oz. marshmallows

Meat and Poultry

6 slices bacon
2 whole chicken breasts
750 g or 1 ½ lb. pork shoulder
  roast
500 g or 1 lb. lean ground beef
450 g or 1 lb. boneless beef sirloin

Fresh Fruits and Vegetables

500 mL or 2 cups fresh spinach
  leaves
800 g or 1 ¾ lb. fresh mushrooms
1 lemon
1.5 kg or 3 lb. carrots
125 g or 4 oz. snow peas
2 kg or 4 lb. potatoes
500 mL or 2 cups bean sprouts
2 tomatoes
1 bunch parsley
1 green pepper
2 small or 1 large bunch broccoli
1 small bunch each red and green
  grapes
2 oranges
1 bunch green onions
2 zucchini (18 cm or 7 inch)

Dairy Products

1 doz. eggs
250 mL or 1 cup Parmesan cheese
450 g or 4 oz. whipped cream
  cheese
2 L or 2 qt. milk
185 mL or 6 oz. cream cheese
50 g or 2 oz. Swiss cheese
28 g or 1 oz. Cheddar or Colby
  cheese
250 mL or 1 cup whipping cream

Frozen Foods

500 g or 1 lb. sole fillets
500 mL or 2 cups French-style
  green beans
1 pkg (280 g or 10 oz.) peas
1 small can orange juice

Bread

3 slices white bread

Miscellaneous

10 mL or 2 tsp. sunflower or
  sesame seeds
200 g or 7 oz. fettuccini
1 mL or ¼ tsp. seasoned salt
300 mL or 1 ¼ cup oatmeal
125 mL or ½ cup coconut
125 mL or ½ cup pecans
5 mL or 1 tsp. soy sauce
50 mL or ¼ tsp. oyster sauce
  (substitute soy if not available)
1 pkg unflavoured gelatin
75 mL or ⅓ cup solid shortening
175 mL or ⅔ cup molasses
500 mL or 2 cups icing sugar
5 mL or 1 tsp. instant coffee
50 mL or ¼ cup cider vinegar
125 mL or ½ cup raisins
500 mL or 2 cups long grain rice
300 mL or 1 ¼ cups graham
  crumbs

Wine or Liquor

25 mL or 2 Tbsp. dry white wine
15 mL or 1 Tbsp. orange liqueur
50 mL or ¼ cup Kahlua liqueur

WEEK 3

Canned Goods

1 can (540 mL or 19 oz.) dark
  sweet cherries
1 can (540 mL or 19 oz.) crushed
  pineapple
2 cans (213 g or 7.5 oz.) salmon
1 can (540 mL or 19 oz.) tomatoes

Meat, Fish, Poultry

2 whole chicken breasts
2 slices ham
350 g or 12 oz. boneless beef
  sirloin
50 g or 2 oz. prosciutto
4 ham steaks
500 g or 1 lb. lean ground beef
1 frying chicken

Fresh Fruits and Vegetables

1 bunch green onions
1 bunch parsley
2 kg or 4.5 lb. potatoes
625 g or 20 oz. zucchini (about
  3 zucchini 18 cm or 7 inch long)
1 green pepper
1 apple
500 g or 1 lb. fresh mushrooms
1 lemon
1 pkg (280 g or 10 oz.) spinach
1 bunch broccoli
assorted fresh fruit to make
  4 servings

Dairy Products

100 g or 3 oz. Swiss cheese
125 g or 4 oz. Parmesan cheese
1 doz. eggs
450 g or 1 lb. butter
1 L or 1 qt. milk
125 mL or ½ cup sour cream
250 mL or 1 cup half and half or
  cereal cream

Frozen Foods

500 mL or 2 cups French-style
  green beans
500 mL or 1 pint vanilla ice cream
375 g or 12 oz. peas

Bread

12 white crackers
6 slices brown bread

Miscellaneous

50 mL or ¼ cup bread crumbs
25 mL or 2 Tbsp. dark soy sauce
50 mL or ¼ cup molasses
375 g or 12 oz. noodles
30 mL or 2 Tbsp. dried vegetable
  flakes
125 mL or ½ cup coconut
50 mL or ¼ cup orange
  marmalade
125 mL or ½ cup raisins
250 mL or 1 cup cornflakes
30 mL or 2 Tbsp. prepared
  horseradish
30 mL or 2 Tbsp. sesame seeds
30 mL or 2 Tbsp. mayonnaise

Wine or Liquor

125 mL or ½ cup white wine
45 mL or ¼ cup orange liqueur
50 mL or ¼ cup rum

STAPLE LIST — check to be sure
   adequate amounts are on hand

salt	cream of tartar
pepper	baking powder
curry powder	baking soda
garlic salt	white sugar
cinnamon	brown sugar
paprika	cornstarch
thyme	flour
white pepper	cocoa
bay leaves	almond extract
dry mustard	vanilla
dried parsley	oil
basil	onions
oregano	garlic cloves
savory	ketchup
whole cloves	bottled lemon juice
ginger	beef bouillon powder or cubes
rosemary	chicken bouillon powder or cubes
nutmeg	long grain rice

Serves 4

Cornish Game Hens with Crab Stuffing (p. 83)
Wild Rice Medley (p. 119)
Brussels Sprouts with Herb Cheese Sauce (p. 104)
Green Salad with Bacon Dressing (p. 185)
Zabaglione (p. 147)

PLAN OF ACTION:

Two hours or the night before serving time:
1. Prepare and cook Bacon Dressing. Store in refrigerator.
2. Prepare Wild Rice Medley, cooking for 35 minutes instead of 40. Leave covered and store in refrigerator.
3. Prepare stuffing for Cornish Game Hens. Cover and store in refrigerator or keep warm.

Approximately 1 hour before serving time:
1. Heat rice on HIGH for 5 minutes or until heated through, stirring several times. Keep warm. While rice is heating prepare Cornish Game Hens.
2. Cook Cornish hens. While hens are cooking prepare Brussels Sprouts and Herb Cheese Sauce. Prepare salad greens.
3. Cook sprouts followed by sauce. While sprouts cook prepare Zabaglione. Pour dressing over greens. If dressing is chilled micro-cook on LOW (30%) for 1 minute to warm slightly.
4. After dinner cook Zabaglione.

Serves 4

Seafood Stuffed Chicken Breasts (p. 71)
Carottes à l'Orange (p. 106)
Buttered Noodles
Brazilian Banana Cake (p. 152)

PLAN OF ACTION:

One hour or the night before serving time:
1. Prepare and cook Brazilian Banana Cake through step 3.

Approximately 30-45 minutes before serving time:
1. Peel carrots and let soak while preparing Seafood Stuffed Chicken Breasts.
2. Micro-cook noodles: Place 1.5 L (6 cups) hot salted water in a 3 L (3 qt.) microwave container. Micro-cook on HIGH (100%) until boiling. Add 375 g (12 oz.) noodles and micro-cook on HIGH (100%) for 8-10 minutes or until tender. Drain and rinse with hot water. Stir in 15 mL (1 Tbsp.) butter to coat.
OR cook noodles conventionally on stove while chicken is cooking.
3. Finish preparing and cook Carottes à l'Orange.
4. Cook chicken.
5. After dinner whip cream and assemble cake (step 4.). (OR whip cream just before dinner and hold in refrigerator. Then assemble cake after dinner.)

Serves 4

Creamy Carrot Soup (p. 46)
Grilled Salmon (p. 84)
Parsley Rice (p. 117)
Broccoli with Hollandaise Sauce (p. 102)
Easy Fruit Flan (p. 139)

Salmon is beautiful done in the microwave and it makes a quick meal either for company or family.

PLAN OF ACTION:

One to two hours or the night before serving time:
1. Prepare and cook Fruit Flan.
2. Prepare and cook Parsley Rice cooking 10 minutes instead of 12 minutes. Do not add parsley. Cover and store in refrigerator or keep warm.
3. Prepare and cook Creamy Carrot Soup and store in refrigerator or keep warm.

Approximately 30 minutes before serving time:
1. If prepared the night before reheat rice on HIGH for 4 minutes or until hot and stir in parsley. Keep warm.
2. If prepared the night before reheat soup. Keep warm.
3. Prepare and cook Grilled Salmon. Meanwhile prepare Broccoli and Hollandaise Sauce.
4. Cook broccoli.
5. Cook Hollandaise sauce.

Serves 4

Stuffed Mushrooms (p. 42)
Pork Loin Teriyaki (p. 64)
Potatoes and Sour Cream (p. 124)
Carrot Celery Medley (p. 107)
Maple Trifle (p. 150)

PLAN OF ACTION:

The night before serving time:
1. Prepare and cook Maple Trifle through step 3.
2. Prepare Potatoes in Sour Cream. Cover and chill in refrigerator.
3. Make marinade for Pork Loin Teriyaki and marinate roast.

Approximately 50 minutes before serving time:
1. Cook roast. While roast is cooking prepare Stuffed Mushrooms and Celery Carrot Medley
2. Cook mushrooms and serve. If using the barbecue put roast over coals while serving mushrooms.
3. Cook potatoes increasing time on LOW (30%) to 5 minutes if prepared the night before.
4. Cook Celery Carrot Medley.
5. After dinner whip cream and garnish cake (step 4).

Serves 8

Rolled Stuffed Roast (p. 54)
Gratinée of Cauliflower (p. 108)
Broccoli with Sesame Seed Butter (p. 102)
Fresh Linguine
Gâteau Allemande Framboise (p. 151)

Stuffing an otherwise ordinary cut of meat makes it elegant enough for an important dinner party. Tender cuts of meat cook very quickly in the microwave so this "roast" will serve 8 people yet require only 12 minutes of actual cooking time. Some time is required to make the stuffing, but this can be done ahead.

The Gâteau Allemande Fraise is a perfect light desert to serve with raspberries and whipped cream for an elegant finish to a meal.

PLAN OF ACTION:

Two hours or the night before serving time:
1. Prepare and cook Gâteau Allemande through step 5.

Approximately 1 ½ hours before serving time:
1. Make the stuffing for the Rolled Stuffed Roast. Prepare and cook roast. Cover and let stand. While roast is cooking start salted water heating on regular stove for pasta.
2. Prepare and cook Gratinée of Cauliflower to end of step 3. Cover and let stand.
3. Meanwhile cook pasta until just tender.
4. Prepare and cook Broccoli with Sesame Seed Butter.
5. Finish step 4 for cauliflower.
6. After dinner finish cake as in step 6.

Serves 8

Hot Spiced Punch (p. 44)
Creamy Ham Scallop (p. 66)
Golden Potato Balls (p. 121)
Bacon Cornmeal Muffins (p. 181)
Lemon Cream Layers (p. 130)

An easy menu to serve 8 people requiring a minimum of preparation time.
PLAN OF ACTION:

The night before serving time:
1. Make Lemon Cream Layers and chill in refrigerator.
2. Prepare and cook Ham Scallop through step 3. Cover and store in refrigerator.
3. Make Hot Spiced Punch and store in refrigerator.

Approximately 30 minutes before serving time:
1. Finish Ham Scallop heating 6-8 minutes or until heated through stirring several times. While ham is heating prepare Cornbread Muffins
2. Cook muffins.
3. Prepare and cook a double recipe of Golden Potato Balls.
4. Reheat punch.

Fresh Fruit
California Quiche
Toasted English Muffin Bread with Jam

Fresh Fruit
California Quiche (p. 95)
Toasted English Muffin Bread (p. 183)
Strawberry Jam (p. 189)

Serves 12

Crab or Spinach Dip with Crackers and Vegetables (p. 39)
Lasagne (p. 57)
Green Salad   Crusty Rolls
Apricot Cake (p. 164)

These recipes are real crowd pleasers and all can be made ahead of time. The dips can be stored several days in the refrigerator. The Apricot Cake can be made well in advance, up to a day before serving and the lasagne is much better if prepared a day ahead and reheated at serving time.

Serves 12

Barbecue Beef Brisket (p. 55)
Scalloped Potatoes (p. 125)
Vegetable Mornay (p. 115)
Frozen Chocolate Tortoni Torte (p. 136)

Beef brisket makes a flavourful dish to serve a large crowd. Since it is a tough cut of meat, it requires a relatively long time to cook. This can be done well ahead of the serving time and becomes even more flavourful on reheating. The scalloped potatoes could also be made ahead and reheated if that helps your meal planning. The frozen torte is served directly from the freezer and can easily be made several days ahead.

PLAN OF ACTION:

The night before:
1. Prepare Frozen Chocolate Tortoni Torte and freeze.
2. Prepare Barbecue Beef Brisket through step 2. Cover and store in refrigerator.

Approximately 1 hour before serving time:
1. Prepare Scalloped Potatoes, tripling the recipe. Use a 3 L (12 cup) tube pan. Cover and micro-cook on HIGH (100%) for 10 minutes and LOW (30%) for 30 minutes.
2. Prepare Vegetable Mornay, tripling the recipe. Double all times and check for doneness. More time may be required.

Fruit Soup or Fresh Fruit in Season (p. 45)
Spanish Eggs (p. 93)
Bacon Cornmeal Muffins (p. 181)

PLAN OF ACTION:

45 minutes or the night before serving time:
1. Prepare fruit and store in refrigerator.

Approximately 30 minutes before serving time:
1. Prepare sauce for Spanish Eggs. Let stand.
2. Prepare and cook Bacon Corn Muffins.
3. Cook eggs in sauce.

Curried Stewed Fruit (p. 45)
Eggs Benedict (p. 94)
Sunday Streusel Coffee Cake (p. 182)

PLAN OF ACTION:

One hour or the night before serving time:
1. Prepare and cook Curried Stewed Fruit and store in refrigerator.
2. Prepare dry ingredients for Sunday Streusel Coffee Cake.

30 minutes before serving time:
1. Finish preparing and cook coffee cake.
2. Prepare Eggs Benedict.

Fresh Fruit with Grand Marnier Sauce (p. 191)
Swiss Breakfast Pie (p. 94)

PLAN OF ACTION:

30 minutes or the night before serving time:
1. Prepare and cook Grand Marnier Sauce.

Approximately 20 minutes before serving time:
1. Prepare and cook Swiss Breakfast Pie. While pie is cooking prepare fruit.

Fresh Fruit in Season
California Quiche (p. 95)
English Muffin Bread and Strawberry Jam (p. 183, 189)

PLAN OF ACTION:

Strawberry Jam can be made whenever convenient, either from fresh or frozen berries.

The night before serving time:
1. Prepare and cook English Muffin Bread.
2. Prepare and cook pie crust for California Quiche. While crust is cooking prepare fruit.
3. Cook bacon for quiche.

Approximately 30 minutes before serving time:
1. Prepare and cook California Quiche.
2. Slice bread. Toast and butter.

BEGINNINGS

Appetizers
Beverages
Soups

Crab Dip

Makes 300 mL (1 ¼ cups)

250 g	cream cheese	8 oz.
1 can(156 mL)	crab	1 can(5 oz.)
50 mL	mayonnaise or salad dressing	¼ cup
5 mL	ketchup	1 tsp.
30 mL	finely chopped onion	2 Tbsp.
5 mL	horseradish	1 tsp.
5 mL	lemon juice	1 tsp.

1. In a microwavable container micro-cook cream cheese on LOW (30%) for 1 minute to soften.
2. Drain and flake crab. Combine all ingredients.
3. Micro-cook on MEDIUM (70%) for 3 minutes stirring once until hot. Serve with crackers or assorted raw vegetables.

1 Serving — 15 mL (1 Tbsp.)

Calories	67	Carbohydrate	1 g
Protein	2 g	Cholesterol	24 mg
Fat	6 g	Sodium	69 mg

Spinach Dip

Makes 675 mL (2 ½ cups)

1 pkg.(280 g)	frozen chopped spinach	1 pkg.(10 oz.)
125 mL	chopped fresh parsley	½ cup
125 mL	finely chopped green onion	½ cup
2 mL	seasoning salt	½ tsp.
10 mL	lemon juice	2 tsp.
250 mL	sour cream	1 cup
250 mL	mayonnaise or salad dressing	1 cup
1 mL	salt	¼ tsp.

1. Place spinach in a microwavable colander. Defrost on defrost program approximately 10 minutes. Press out moisture thoroughly. Chop finely or purée in a food processor or blender.
2. Combine with remaining ingredients.

1 Serving — 15 mL (1 Tbsp.)

Calories	54	Carbohydrate	1 g
Protein	1 g	Cholesterol	13 mg
Fat	6 g	Sodium	79 mg

Artichoke Dip

Makes 500 mL (2 cups)

1 can(398 mL)	artichokes, not marinated	1 can(14 oz.)
125 mL	mayonnaise or salad dressing	1/2 cup
125 mL	sour cream or yogurt	1/2 cup
250 mL	grated Parmesan cheese	1 cup

1. Drain artichokes and chop finely. Combine with mayonnaise and cheese in a 750 mL (3 cup) microwavable container. Micro-cook on MEDIUM (70%) for 2 minutes, stir and micro-cook 1 minute longer or until heated through. Serve with crackers or assorted raw vegetables.

1 Serving — 15 mL (1 Tbsp.)

Calories	47	Carbohydrate	1 g
Protein	1 g	Cholesterol	10 mg
Fat	4 g	Sodium 98 mg	

Chili Con Questo Dip

Makes 500 mL (2 cups)

3 slices	bacon, chopped	3 slices
1	small onion, finely chopped	1
1 can(540 mL)	tomatoes	1 can(19 oz.)
1 can(114 mL)	jalapeno peppers, drained and chopped	1 can(4 oz.)
250 g	Monterey Jack or Farmers cheese grated	8 oz.

1. Micro-cook bacon in a 1 L (4 cup) microwavable container on HIGH (100 %) for 1 minute, drain. Add onion and micro-cook on HIGH (100 %) for 2 minutes or until onion is soft.
2. Drain tomatoes and stir into onion mixture. Add peppers and cheese. Process in a food processor or blender until smooth. Micro-cook on MEDIUM (70%) for 4 to 5 minutes until cheese is melted. Stir well.
Serve with tortilla chips.
Note: This dip is quite hot. Use fewer peppers for a milder flavour.

1 Serving — 15 mL (1 Tbsp.)

Calories	66	Carbohydrate	1 g
Protein	2 g	Cholesterol	12 mg
Fat	6 g	Sodium	131 mg

Ham Puffs

12 appetizers

75 mL	flaked cooked ham	$1/3$ cup
5 mL	chopped green onion or chives	1 tsp.
50 mL	mayonnaise	$1/4$ cup
15 mL	green pickle relish	1 Tbsp.
1	egg white	1
	grated Parmesan cheese	
	paprika	
12	Melba Toast rounds	12

1. Combine ham, green onion, mayonnaise, and relish.
2. Beat egg white until stiff and fold in.
3. Drop mixture by teaspoonsful onto crisp crackers. Top with grated cheese and a dash of paprika.
4. Place crackers in a circle on a ridged microwavable serving plate or rack. Micro-cook on HIGH (100 %) for 1 to 1 $1/4$ minutes. Serve hot.

1 Serving	Calories	54	Carbohydrate	2 g
	Protein	2 g	Cholesterol	10 mg
	Fat	5 g	Sodium	101 mg

Bacon Melts

12 appetizers

3 slices	bacon, diced	3 slices
75 mL	shredded Cheddar cheese	$1/3$ cup
25 mL	mayonnaise	2 Tbsp.
2 mL	chopped fresh parsley	$1/2$ tsp.
2 mL	poppy seeds	$1/2$ tsp.
12	Melba Toast rounds	12

1. Place bacon in small microwavable container and micro-cook on HIGH (100 %) until crisp, stirring several times. Drain on paper towel.
2. Combine bacon with cheese, mayonnaise, parsley and poppy seeds. Place a small spoonful on each cracker. Arrange crackers in a circle on a ridged microwavable plate or rack. Micro-cook on HIGH (100 %) just until cheese is melted, about 40 seconds. Serve hot.

1 Serving	Calories	49	Carbohydrate	1 g
	Protein	2 g	Cholesterol	9 mg
	Fat	4 g	Sodium	68 mg

Cocktail Almonds

Makes 500 mL (2 cups)

30 mL	butter	2 Tbsp.
1 mL	garlic salt	1/4 tsp.
1 mL	salt	1/4 tsp.
500 mL	blanched whole almonds	2 cups

1. Melt butter in shallow microwavable container on HIGH (100 %)
for 30 seconds.
2. Mix in salts. Toss with nuts. Micro-cook on HIGH (100 %) for
5 to 6 minutes, stirring occasionally until nuts are light brown.

1 Serving — 50 mL (1/4 cup)	Calories	115	Carbohydrate	3 g
	Protein	3 g	Cholesterol	8 mg
	Fat	10 g	Sodium	151 mg

Stuffed Mushrooms

18 appetizers

18	large fresh mushrooms	18
50 mL	butter	1/4 cup
4	green onions, finely chopped	4
1 mL	garlic salt	1/4 tsp.
1 mL	dried parsley	1/4 tsp.
1 mL	dry mustard	1/4 tsp.
1 mL	dried oregano	1/4 tsp.
5 mL	soy sauce	1 tsp.
50 mL	grated Parmesan cheese	1/4 cup
50 mL	dry bread crumbs	1/4 cup

1. Brush mushrooms and remove stems. Finely chop stems.
2. In a 750 mL (3 cup) microwavable container micro-cook butter on
HIGH (100 %) until melted, about 30 seconds. Add chopped stems
and green onion. Micro-cook on HIGH (100 %) 2 minutes or until
soft. Stir in remaining ingredients and micro-cook on HIGH (100 %)
for 1 minute.
3. Stuff caps and arrange in a circle on a flat microwavable dish.
Micro-cook on HIGH (100 %) just until hot, about 3 minutes.

1 Serving	Calories	50	Carbohydrate	2 g
	Protein	1 gm	Cholesterol	11 mg
	Fat	4 gm	Sodium	116 mg

Bacon Sticks

8 appetizers

8 slices	**bacon**	**8 slices**
8	**unsalted bread sticks**	**8**

1. Place bacon on a microwavable bacon rack, cover with a paper towel and micro-cook on HIGH (100 %) for 4 minutes.
2. Wrap each bread stick with a strip of bacon and place on bacon rack. Cover with a paper towel and micro-cook on HIGH (100 %) for 2 $\frac{1}{2}$ to 3 $\frac{1}{2}$ minutes or until bacon is crisp.

1 Serving				
	Calories	60 g	Carbohydrate	2 g
	Protein	3 g	Cholesterol	7 mg
	Fat	5 g	Sodium	146 mg

Zucchini Appetizers

20 appetizers

2-3	**small zucchini**	**2-3**
75 mL	**mayonnaise**	**$\frac{1}{3}$ cup**
50 mL	**minced green onions**	**$\frac{1}{4}$ cup**
75 mL	**grated Parmesan cheese**	**$\frac{1}{3}$ cup**
dash	**pepper**	**dash**
2 mL	**oregano**	**$\frac{1}{2}$ tsp.**
0.5 mL	**garlic powder**	**$\frac{1}{8}$ tsp.**
50 mL	**fine dry bread crumbs**	**$\frac{1}{4}$ cup**
	paprika	

1. Cut zucchini into a total of 20 equal slices. Place slices in a single layer on a flat microwavable dish. Cover with parchment or wax paper. Micro-cook on HIGH (100%) for 3 minutes or until zucchini gives slightly when gently squeezed. Use a paper towel to absorb moisture from top of zucchini
2. In a small bowl combine mayonnaise, onions, cheese, pepper, oregano and garlic powder. Blend well. Spoon mixture evenly on each zucchini slice.
3. Sprinkle tops with bread crumbs and then a dash of paprika.
4. Arrange half the zucchini slices in a circle on a flat microwavable plate. Micro-cook, uncovered, on HIGH (100%) for 1 minute or until heated through. Repeat with remaining slices. Let stand 3 minutes before serving.

1 Appetizer				
	Calories	37	Carbohydrate	1 g
	Protein	7 g	Cholesterol	3 mg
	Fat	3 g	Sodium	50 mg

Hot Spiced Punch

Makes 1.5 L (6 cups)

1 L	apple juice or cider	4 cups
500 mL	orange juice	2 cups
	juice of 1 lemon	
2	cinnamon sticks	2
15 mL	whole cloves	1 Tbsp.
5 mL	allspice	1 tsp.
pinch	nutmeg	pinch
175 mL	honey	2/3 cup

1. Combine all ingredients in a 3 L (3 qt.) microwavable container. Micro-cook on HIGH (100 %) until boiling, then on LOW (30%) for 5 minutes. Strain and serve in cups.

1 Serving — 125 mL (½ cup)

Calories	87	Carbohydrate	22 g
Protein	0	Cholesterol	0 mg
Fat	0	Sodium	5 mg

Mulled Wine

Makes 1 L (4 cups)

125 mL	water	1/2 cup
30 mL	honey	2 Tbsp.
6	whole cloves	6
3	whole allspice	3
dash	nutmeg	dash
1	cinnamon stick	1
	rind of 1/2 lemon	
1 L	red wine	32 oz.
125 mL	port wine	1/2 cup

1. Combine water, honey, spices and lemon rind in a 3 L (3 qt.) microwavable container. Cover and micro-cook on HIGH (100 %) for 5 minutes or until boiling then on LOW (30%) for 10 minutes.
2. Stir in wine and port. Micro-cook on MEDIUM (70%) just until hot. Do not allow to boil. Garnish with lemon slices.

1 Serving — 125 mL (½ cup)

Calories	109	Carbohydrate	8 g
Protein	0	Cholesterol	0 mg
Fat	0	Sodium	6 mg

Curried Stewed Fruit

Serves 4

2	small oranges, peeled and sliced	2
250 mL	chopped prunes	1 cup
75 mL	raisins	1/3 cup
250 mL	apple juice	1 cup
15 mL	honey	1 Tbsp.
dash	curry powder	dash
1	apple, peeled, cored and sliced	1

1. Place all ingredients except apple in 1 L (1 qt.) microwavable container. Micro-cook on HIGH (100%) for 5 minutes. Add apple and micro-cook on HIGH (100%) for 1 minute longer.

1 serving	Calories	218	Carbohydrate	37 g
	Protein	2 g	Cholesterol	0 mg
	Fat	0 g	Sodium	7 mg

Fruit Soup

Serves 4

300 g	mixed dried fruit	12 oz.
375 mL	water	1 1/2 cups
375 mL	grape juice	1 1/2 cups
1/2	lemon, sliced	1/2
15 mL	tapioca	1 Tbsp.
1 mL	salt	1/4 tsp.
125 mL	sugar	1/2 cup
1	stick cinnamon	1

1. Combine all ingredients in a 2 L (2 qt.) microwavable container and micro-cook on HIGH (100%) until boiling, about 10 minutes. Micro-cook on LOW (30%) for 5 minutes longer or until fruit is tender. Serve hot or cold.

1 serving	Calories	420	Carbohydrate	109 g
	Protein	3 g	Cholesterol	0 mg
	Fat	1 g	Sodium	133 mg

Creamy Carrot Soup

Serves 6-8

The delicious flavour of this soup comes from the port wine. Adding cottage cheese gives a creamy consistency without using higher calorie cream.

30 mL	butter	2 Tbsp.
250 mL	chopped onions	1 cup
500 g	carrots, peeled and sliced	1 lb.
2 mL	salt	1/2 tsp.
	freshly ground black pepper	
1L	chicken stock	4 cups
50 mL	cottage or ricotta cheese	1/4 cup
30 mL	port wine	2 Tbsp.

1. In a 3 L (3 qt.) microwavable container combine butter and onions. Micro-cook on HIGH (100 %) for 2-3 minutes or until onions are soft. Add carrots, salt, pepper and chicken stock. Micro-cook on HIGH (100%) for 10 minutes or until boiling. Reduce power to LOW (30%) and micro-cook for 15 minutes or until carrots are soft.
2. Add cottage cheese and wine and place in blender or food processor. Process until smooth. Reheat if necessary. Serve hot or cold garnished with dill.

Note: If using a food processor drain off liquid and purée vegetables separately, then mix together.

1 Serving				
	Calories	100	Carbohydrate	6 g
	Protein	4 g	Cholesterol	10 mg
	Fat	6 g	Sodium	233 mg

Easy Vegetable Soup

Serves 6-8

450 g	ground beef	1 lb.
125 mL	chopped onion	1/2 cup
30 mL	beef bouillon powder	2 Tbsp.
125 mL	uncooked macaroni	1/2 cup
1 L	chopped vegetables — carrots, celery, zucchini, cabbage etc.	4 cups
1 can(540mL)	tomatoes	1 can(19 oz.)
5 mL	salt	1 tsp.
2 mL	thyme	1/2 tsp.
	hot water	

1. Brown meat in bottom of a 3 L (3 qt.) microwavable container with lid on HIGH (100 %) for 3 to 4 minutes or until slightly pink. Stir several times to crumble. Drain off fat.
2. Add onion and micro-cook on HIGH (100 %) for 2 minutes.
3. Add bouillon, macaroni, vegetables, tomatoes, salt and thyme. Add enough hot water to come to within 2.5 cm (1 inch) of top of pot. Cover and micro-cook on HIGH (100 %) for 12 minutes, stir and then micro-cook on MEDIUM-LOW (50%) for 15 minutes longer or until vegetables are almost tender. Let stand 10 minutes.

1 Serving					
	Calories	152	Carbohydrate	11 g	
	Protein	13 g	Cholesterol	28 mg	
	Fat	6 g	Sodium	593 mg	

Clam Chowder

Serves 4-6

An easy, tasty soup for a cold winter evening.

5 slices	bacon, diced	5 slices
1-2	onions, diced	1-2
50 mL	flour	1/4 cup
1L	milk or cream	4 cups
3	potatoes, diced	3
5 mL	thyme	1 tsp.
1 can(142g)	clams	1 can(5 oz.)

1. In a 3 L (3 qt.) microwavable casserole micro-cook bacon on HIGH (100 %) for 5 minutes or until crisp stirring several times. Add onions and micro-cook on HIGH (100 %) for 2 minutes or until tender. Stir in flour.
2. Blend in milk, potatoes and thyme. Micro-cook on HIGH (100 %) for 10 minutes or until boiling and then on LOW (30%) for 10 minutes or until potatoes are tender. Stir in clams with juice.

1 Serving					
	Calories	302	Carbohydrate	28 g	
	Protein	14 g	Cholesterol	43 mg	
	Fat	15 g	Sodium	257 mg	

Cream of Mushroom Soup

Serves 4-6

250 g	fresh mushrooms	8 oz.
25 mL	butter	2 Tbsp.
1	medium onion, finely chopped	1
50 mL	butter	1/4 cup
50 mL	flour	1/4 cup
250 mL	light cream or milk	1 cup
750 mL	chicken broth	3 cups
2 mL	salt	1/2 tsp.
dash	pepper	dash
25 mL	sherry	2 Tbsp.

1. Brush mushrooms and slice thinly.
2. In a 750 mL (3 cup) microwavable container melt first amount butter on HIGH (100 %) for 30 seconds. Add mushrooms and chopped onion. Micro-cook on HIGH (100 %) for 5 minutes, stirring once.
3. In a 3 L (3 qt.) microwavable container melt second amount of butter on HIGH (100 %) for 1 minute. Stir in flour. Blend in cream and 250 mL (1 cup) chicken broth. Micro-cook on HIGH (100%) until thickened and boiling, about 5 minutes. Stir after 3 minutes. Stir in mushroom mixture and remaining chicken broth. Season to taste. When ready to serve stir in sherry and heat at MEDIUM (70%) about 5 minutes. Stir well and serve.

1 Serving				
	Calories	307	Carbohydrate	9 g
	Protein	7 g	Cholesterol	66 mg
	Fat	28 g	Sodium	413 mg

MAIN DISHES

Beef
Pork
Lamb
Poultry
Fish & Seafood
Eggs

Beef Stroganoff

Serves 4

An easy version of an old favorite.

25 mL	butter	2 Tbsp.
125 mL	chopped onion	1/2 cup
350 g	beef sirloin, thinly sliced	12 oz.
250 mL	sliced fresh mushrooms	1 cup
5 mL	instant beef bouillon	1 tsp.
1 mL	salt	1/4 tsp.
30 mL	flour	2 Tbsp.
75 mL	water	1/3 cup
125 mL	white wine	1/2 cup
125 mL	sour cream	1/2 cup

1. Melt butter in a 1 L (4 cup) microwavable casserole on HIGH (100%) for 30 seconds. Add onion and micro-cook on HIGH (100%) for 1 minute.
2. Stir in meat and mushrooms and micro-cook on HIGH (100%) for 5 minutes just until meat loses its pink colour, stirring once.
3. Combine bouillon, salt and flour with water. Stir into meat mixture. Stir in wine. Micro-cook on HIGH (100%) for 4 minutes or until boiling, stirring several times.
4. Stir in sour cream and serve over hot noodles.

1 serving				
	Calories	269	Carbohydrate	7 g
	Protein	23 g	Cholesterol	85 mg
	Fat	16 g	Sodium	469 mg

Green Pepper Steak

Serves 4

450 g	sirloin tip steak	1 lb.
50 mL	light soy sauce	1/4 cup
15 mL	cornstarch	1 Tbsp.
5 mL	ground ginger	1 tsp.
dash	garlic powder	dash
30 mL	oil	2 Tbsp.
2	green peppers, cut in chunks	2
2	onions, sliced	2

1. Cut steak into thin strips.
2. Combine soy sauce, cornstarch and seasonings. Marinate steak for 20 to 30 minutes.
3. Preheat a large browning dish on HIGH (100%) for 6 minutes. Immediately add oil and then meat and marinade. Stir until sizzle stops.
4. Stir in peppers and onions. Cover and micro-cook on HIGH (100%) for 7 minutes or until peppers are tender-crisp. Let stand 1 to 2 minutes.

1 serving				
	Calories	285	Carbohydrate	12 g
	Protein	28 g	Cholesterol	61 mg
	Fat	14 g	Sodium	1065 mg

Saucy Baked Steak

Serves 4

15 mL	oil	1 Tbsp.
500 g	top round steak cut in 4 pieces	1 lb.
125 mL	Barbecue sauce (page 193)	1/2 cup
50 mL	water	1/4 cup

1. Preheat a large browning dish on HIGH (100%) for 6 minutes. Add oil. Place steak in dish, brown a few seconds and turn over.
2. Combine barbecue sauce and water and pour over meat. Cover. Micro-cook on HIGH (100%) for 5 minutes, then on LOW (30%) for 40 minutes or until tender. Turn meat over halfway through cooking.

1 serving				
	Calories	235	Carbohydrate	6 g
	Protein	26 g	Cholesterol	65 mg
	Fat	11 g	Sodium	371 mg

Beef Vegetable Stir-Fry

Serves 4

500 mL	frozen French-style green beans	2 cups
450 g	beef sirloin	1 lb.
5 mL	cornstarch	1 tsp.
5 mL	salt	1 tsp.
5 mL	soy sauce	1 tsp.
15 mL	oil	1 Tbsp.
1	onion, sliced thinly	1
1 clove	garlic, minced	1 clove
250 mL	sliced fresh mushrooms	1 cup
500 mL	fresh bean sprouts	2 cups
50 mL	oyster sauce	$1/4$ cup
30 mL	cornstarch	2 Tbsp.
175 mL	chicken broth*	$3/4$ cup

1. Defrost beans on HIGH (100%) about 2 minutes.
2. Slice beef into thin strips.
3. Combine first amount of cornstarch, salt and soy sauce and stir in beef. Marinate while preparing vegetables.
4. Preheat a large browning dish on HIGH (100%) for 6 minutes. Add oil, then meat. When sizzle stops add onion and garlic. Micro-cook on HIGH (100%) for 2 minutes.
5. Add mushrooms, beans, and bean sprouts. Cover and micro-cook on HIGH (100%) for 2 minutes.
6. Combine oyster sauce, cornstarch, and broth and stir in. Micro-cook on HIGH (100%) for 4 minutes or until sauce is slightly thickened.
Serve over rice.

*Make chicken broth by using 3 mL ($3/4$ tsp.) chicken bouillon powder and 175 mL ($3/4$ cup) water.

Note: Oyster sauce is available in any Chinese food store. It is well worth the effort to obtain, for it gives a nice flavour to the stir-fry. Soy sauce may be substituted.

1 serving					
	Calories	297	Carbohydrate	18 g
	Protein	31 g	Cholesterol	63 mg
	Fat	12 g	Sodium	769 mg

Rolled Stuffed Roast

Serves 8

A nice dish to serve for company — a bit of work, but well worth the effort.

750 g	boneless sirloin steak or sirloin tip steak which butcher has put through a tenderizing machine.	**1 ¹/₂ lb.**
	basil	
	oregano	
2 slices	bacon, diced	2 slices
125 mL	chopped onion	¹/₂ cup
1 clove	garlic, minced	1 clove
1 can(398 mL)	artichokes, drained and chopped	1 can(14 oz.)
2 sprigs	parsley	2 sprigs
3	eggs	3
15 mL	grated Parmesan cheese	1 Tbsp.
125 g	Italian mortadella bologna* thinly sliced	4 oz.
1	small onion, quartered	1
1 mL	rosemary	¹/₄ tsp.
125 mL	dry red wine	¹/₂ cup
	parsley for garnish	

1. With a meat mallet flatten meat to approximately 25 x 33 cm (10x13 in). Sprinkle with basil and oregano.
2. Make Stuffing: Place bacon, onion, and garlic in a 750 mL (3 cup) microwavable container. Cover and micro-cook on HIGH (100%) about 4 minutes stirring once. Add artichokes and parsley. Micro-cook on HIGH (100%) another 2 minutes. Set aside.
3. Make Fritta: Beat eggs and pour into a 25 cm (10 inch) microwavable pie plate. Cover with parchment or wax paper and micro-cook on HIGH (100%) 1 minute. Stir, cover and micro-cook on MEDIUM (70%) another 2-3 minutes or until eggs are well set.
4. Place fritta on meat and sprinkle with basil, oregano and the Parmesan. Place mortadella over the surface. Place the stuffing mixture on top and press gently into a cylindrical shape the width of the meat. Roll meat tightly to make a roast-like shape and tie in four places with heavy string.
5. In a 1.5 L (6 cup) microwavable loaf dish place onion, rosemary and wine. Place roast over onions. Cover with parchment or wax paper and micro-cook on MEDIUM (70%) about 12 minutes, turning after 6 minutes. Cover with foil and allow to stand 10 minutes.
6. Slice carefully and place on a platter. Pour wine sauce over and garnish platter with parsley.
*Mortadella bolgona is available in Italian speciality stores. Regular bologna may be substituted.

1 serving				
	Calories	258	Carbohydrate	4 g
	Protein	26 g	Cholesterol	174 mg
	Fat	15 g	Sodium	356 mg

Barbecue Beef Brisket

Serves 10-12

This is delicious served hot for a large crowd. Plan to shred leftover beef and mix with sauce to serve over buns.

2 kg	brisket point, trimmed	4 lb.
2 mL	salt	1/2 tsp.
1	bay leaf	1
50 mL	butter	1/4 cup
2 medium	onions, chopped	2 medium
2 cloves	garlic, minced	2 cloves
125 mL	chopped celery	1/2 cup
125 mL	water	1/2 cup
500 mL	ketchup	2 cups
50 mL	vinegar	1/4 cup
50 mL	Worcestershire sauce	1/4 cup
50 mL	brown sugar	1/4 cup
2 mL	dry mustard	1/2 tsp.
10 mL	salt	2 tsp.
2 mL	pepper	1/2 tsp.
10 mL	chili powder	2 tsp.
1	bay leaf	1

1. Place brisket in a large microwavable flat pan with lid. Add enough water to almost cover meat. Add first amount of salt and bay leaf making sure salt is dissolved in the water. Cover and micro-cook on HIGH (100%) for 10 minutes or until water is boiling. Then micro-cook on LOW (30%) for 30 minutes. Turn meat over and micro-cook another 40 minutes.

2. In a 750 mL (3 cup) measure melt butter on HIGH. Add onions, garlic, and celery and micro-cook on HIGH (100%) for 3 minutes. Add remaining ingredients and micro-cook on HIGH (100%) for 6 minutes or until boiling and then on MEDIUM (70%) for 4 minutes. Remove bay leaf.

3. Remove meat from pan and slice very thinly. Arrange in a flat baking dish and pour sauce over. Cover and micro-cook on HIGH (100%) for 6 minutes and then on LOW (30%) for 30 minutes longer.

1 serving				
	Calories	360	Carbohydrate	20 g
	Protein	30 g	Cholesterol	116 mg
	Fat	18 g	Sodium	2000 mg

Goulash Hungarian Style

Serves 8

This recipe serves 8 people. Plan to use for two meals, freezing the second portion for a fast meal at a later time.

15 mL	oil	1 Tbsp.
1 kg	stewing beef, cut in cubes	2 lb.
250 mL	thinly sliced onions	1 cup
30 mL	paprika	2 Tbsp.
2 mL	salt	1/2 tsp.
1/2	green pepper, sliced thinly	1/2
50 mL	tomato paste	1/4 cup
dash	cayenne	dash
375 mL	hot water	1 1/2 cup
1 pkt.	instant beef bouillon	1 pkt.
4	medium potatoes, cut in pieces about 2.5cm (1 inch)	4
25 mL	flour	2 Tbsp.
25 mL	water	2 Tbsp.
125 mL	sour cream	1/2 cup

1. Preheat a large browning dish on HIGH (100%) for 6 minutes. Add oil and then meat. Brown until sizzle stops.
2. Add onions, paprika, salt, green pepper, tomato paste, cayenne, hot water and bouillon. Cover and micro-cook on HIGH (100%) for 12 minutes and then on LOW (30%) for 20 minutes.
3. Add potatoes and micro-cook on HIGH (100%) for 1 minute and then on LOW (30%) for 20 minutes. Combine flour and water and stir in. Micro-cook on HIGH (100%) for 1 minute. Let stand 10 minutes and stir in sour cream. Serve over hot noodles.

1 serving				
	Calories	372	Carbohydrate	19 g
	Protein	23 g	Cholesterol	89 mg
	Fat	22 g	Sodium	304 mg

Lasagne

Serves 8

500g	lean ground beef	1 lb.
250 mL	chopped onion	1 cup
1 clove	garlic, minced	1 clove
1 can(796mL)	tomatoes	1 can(28 oz.)
500 mL	tomato juice	2 cups
15 mL	parsley flakes	1 Tbsp.
7 mL	oregano	1 1/2 tsp.
5 mL	basil	1 tsp.
2 mL	salt	1/2 tsp.
1 kg	cottage cheese	2 lb.
2 mL	salt	1/2 tsp.
1	egg	1
15 mL	parsley	1 Tbsp.
50 mL	Parmesan cheese	1/4 cup
375g	Mozzarella cheese	12 oz.
12	uncooked lasagne noodles	12
50 mL	Parmesan cheese	1/4 cup

1. Place beef, onions and garlic in a 3 L (3 qt.) microwavable container and micro-cook on HIGH (100%) for 9 to 10 minutes or until onions are transparent. Stir several times. Drain.
2. Add tomatoes, juice, parsley flakes, oregano, basil and salt and micro-cook uncovered on HIGH (100%) for 5 minutes, then on MEDIUM-LOW (50%) for 20 minutes (less if you are rushed, but the longer time gives better flavour).
3. Combine cottage cheese, salt, egg, parsley flakes, and first amount of Parmesan cheese.
4. Grate Mozzarella cheese. Break noodles to fit two 2 L (2 qt.) microwavable baking pans and layer as follows:
half of noodles
half of sauce
half of cottage cheese mixture
half of Mozzarella
half of noodles
half of sauce
half of cottage cheese mixture
Cover dishes tightly with plastic wrap and stack one dish on top of the other in the oven, turning top dish so it is supported by bottom dish. Micro-cook on MEDIUM-LOW (50%) for 25 minutes. (Reverse dishes halfway through cooking if not cooking evenly).
5. Uncover dishes and add last half of Mozzarella cheese and second amount Parmesan cheese to both dishes. Cook each dish separately on MEDIUM-LOW (50%) for 15 minutes. Cover and allow to stand 20 minutes.

1 serving				
	Calories	381	Carbohydrate	18 g
	Protein	34 g	Cholesterol	105 mg
	Fat	19 g	Sodium	1033 mg

Savory Meatloaf

Serves 4 — 6

Adding shredded vegetables to a meat loaf adds moisture, nutrition and extends the meat. This cuts the cost of your main dish and can encourage children to eat vegetables.

500 g	ground lean beef	1 lb.
250 mL	shredded zucchini or carrot	1 cup
1	small onion, chopped	1
1	egg, beaten	1
50 mL	quick-cooking rolled oats	1/4 cup
50mL	milk	1/4 cup
30 mL	Parmesan cheese	2 Tbsp.
2 mL	oregano or basil	1/2 tsp.
2 mL	instant beef bouillon	1/2 tsp.
dash	pepper	dash
1 mL	salt	1/4 tsp.
15 mL	ketchup	1 Tbsp.

1. Combine all ingredients except ketchup in a mixing bowl and mix well. Press into a 1.5 L (6 cup) microwavable ring mould.
2. Cover with parchment or wax paper and micro-cook on MEDIUM (70%) for 14 to 15 minutes. Let stand approximately 5 minutes. Brush with ketchup.

1 serving				
	Calories	276	Carbohydrate	9 g
	Protein	25 g	Cholesterol	135 mg
	Fat	15 g	Sodium	391 mg

Sweet and Sour Meatballs

Serves 4

500 g	lean ground beef	1 lb.
1	egg	1
50 mL	dry bread crumbs	1/4 cup
5 mL	salt	1 tsp.
1 recipe	Sweet Sour Sauce (page 192)	1 recipe

1. Combine beef with beaten egg, crumbs and salt. Shape into small balls and place in a microwavable rack or dish. Cover with parchment or wax paper and micro-cook on HIGH (100%) for 6 to 8 minutes or until cooked. Drain and combine with sauce. Serve over rice.

1 serving	Calories	415	Carbohydrate	49 g
	Protein	24 g	Cholesterol	132 mg
	Fat	14 g	Sodium	677 mg

Barbecued Meatballs

Make as above except substitute 250 mL (1 cup) Barbecue Sauce from page 193 in place of Sweet Sour Sauce.

1 serving	Calories	301	Carbohydrate	18 g
	Protein	24 g	Cholesterol	132 mg
	Fat	14 g	Sodium	1211 mg

Mexicali Casserole

Serves 4-6

500 g	lean ground beef	1 lb.
1	onion, chopped	1
1	green pepper	1
25 mL	chili powder	2 Tbsp.
1 can(398mL)	corn, drained	1 can(14 oz.)
1 can(398mL)	tomato sauce	1 can(14 oz.)
250 mL	yellow corn meal	1 cup
250 mL	flour	1 cup
25 mL	sugar	2 Tbsp.
20 mL	baking powder	4 tsp.
5 mL	salt	1 tsp.
250 mL	milk	1 cup
1	egg	1
75 mL	oil	1/3 cup

1. Micro-cook meat with onion and green pepper in a flat 2.5 L (2.5 qt.) microwavable casserole or in a large preheated browning dish on HIGH (100%), stirring several times until meat has lost its pink colour. Remove from oven and drain off any fat. Add chili powder, corn and tomato sauce.
2. Preheat conventional or Combination oven to 350°F
3. Combine corn meal, flour, sugar, baking powder and salt. Combine milk, egg and oil. Stir dry mixture into milk mixture and mix only enough to combine. Spread over top of meat mixture in casserole.
4. When oven is preheated, reset to cook on Combination for baked products and cook for 30 to 40 minutes or until top is nicely browned. In a conventional oven, bake at 350°F for 1 hour or until top is browned.

1 serving	Calories	553	Carbohydrate	59 g
	Protein	23 g	Cholesterol	91 mg
	Fat	26 g	Sodium	496 mg

Pizza Casserole

Serves 4

500 mL	uncooked macaroni	2 cups
500 g	ground beef	1 lb.
1	onion, chopped	1
1 jar(398mL)	spaghetti sauce	1 jar(14 oz.)
1 can(280 g)	sliced mushrooms, drained	1 can(10 oz.)
125 mL	sliced pepperoni	1/2 cup
125 g	Mozzarella, grated	4 oz.

1. Place macaroni in a 3 L (3 qt.) microwavable container. Add about 1.5 L (6 cups) hot water and micro-cook on HIGH for 5 minutes or until boiling and then on LOW for 5 minutes. Let stand for 10 minutes. Drain, rinse and set aside.
2. Place beef in a 2 L (2 qt.) microwavable casserole dish and micro-cook on HIGH (100%) for 4 minutes. Stir to crumble and add onion. Micro-cook another 2 to 3 minutes or until meat is no longer pink and onion is tender. Drain.
3. Stir in spaghetti sauce, mushrooms, pepperoni and macaroni. Cover and micro-cook on HIGH (100%) about 6 minutes or until heated through.
4. Sprinkle cheese on top of casserole, cover and let stand 5 minutes.

1 Serving	Calories	607	Carbohydrate	51 g
	Protein	40 g	Cholesterol	91 mg
	Fat	26 g	Sodium	847 mg

Quick Beef-Zucchini Casserole

Serves 4

500 g	ground beef	1 lb.
2 cloves	garlic, minced	2 cloves
1	onion, chopped	1
500 mL	canned tomatoes	2 cups
125 mL	uncooked rice	1/2 cup
50 mL	naturally brewed soy sauce	1/4 cup
5 mL	dried basil	1 tsp.
1 mL	salt	1/4 tsp.
125 mL	hot water	1/2 cup
2	zucchini (approx. 18 cm or 7 in.)	2

1. Place beef, garlic and onion in a 2 L (2 qt.) microwavable casserole. Micro-cook on HIGH (100%) for 5 to 6 minutes or until pink colour is gone. Stir several times. Drain.
2. Slice zucchini thinly and add with remaining ingredients. Cover and micro-cook on HIGH (100%) for 10 minutes, then on LOW (30%) for 15 minutes. Stir twice. Let stand 5 minutes.

1 serving	Calories	346	Carbohydrate	32 g
	Protein	26 g	Cholesterol	57 mg
	Fat	13 g	Sodium	1338 mg

Spaghetti in a Pot

Serves 4

500 g	lean ground beef	1 lb.
125 mL	chopped onion	1/2 cup
1 clove	garlic, minced	1 clove
5 mL	salt	1 tsp.
1 mL	pepper	1/4 tsp.
5 mL	oregano	1 tsp.
2 mL	parsley	1/2 tsp.
2 mL	basil	1/2 tsp.
30 mL	tomato paste	2 Tbsp.
1 can(398 mL)	tomato sauce	1 can(14 oz.)
500 mL	hot water	2 cups
200 g	spaghetti, uncooked	7 oz.
	grated Parmesan cheese	

1. Place beef, onion and garlic in a 2 L (2 qt.) microwavable casserole. Micro-cook on HIGH (100%) for 5-6 minutes, or until beef is no longer pink. Stir several times during cooking.
2. Add salt, pepper, herbs, tomato paste, tomato sauce and water. Cover and micro-cook on HIGH (100%) for 8 minutes or until boiling.
3. Break spaghetti in half and stir into sauce. Cover and micro-cook on HIGH (100%) for 4 minutes. Stir. Cover and micro-cook on MEDIUM-LOW (50%) for 10 minutes. Stir and sprinkle with Parmesan cheese. Let stand 5 minutes.

1 serving				
	Calories	469	Carbohydrate	45 g
	Protein	29 g	Cholesterol	81 mg
	Fat	19 g	Sodium	709 mg

Chili

Serves 4

500 g	ground beef	1 lb.
1	medium onion, chopped	1
1	green pepper, seeded and chopped	1
1	clove garlic, minced	1
30 mL	chili powder	2 Tbsp.
5 mL	cumin	1 tsp.
5 mL	salt	1 tsp.
1 mL	pepper	1/4 tsp.
1 can(213 mL)	tomato sauce	1 can(7.5 oz.)
1 can(796 mL)	tomatoes	1 can(28 oz.)
1 can(540 mL)	kidney beans	1 can(19 oz.)
1 can(540 mL)	white beans	1 can(19 oz.)

1. Place beef, onion, green pepper and garlic in a 3 L (3 qt.) microwavable container. Micro-cook on HIGH (100%) for 5 to 6 minutes or until beef is browned and vegetables are tender. Stir several times. Drain.
2. Add remaining ingredients, cover and and micro-cook for 10 minutes on HIGH (100%) and then for 20 minutes on MEDIUM-LOW (50%), or longer if time permits as the flavour improves with longer cooking.

1 Serving				
	Calories	565	Carbohydrate	68 g
	Protein	43 g	Cholesterol	57 mg
	Fat	15 g	Sodium	932 mg

Pork Loin Teriyaki

Serves 6

A nice roast to finish on your barbecue in the summertime.

125 mL	light soy sauce	1/2 cup
50 mL	dry sherry	1/4 cup
50 mL	honey	1/4 cup
1	clove garlic, crushed	1
10 mL	ground ginger	2 tsp.
1 kg	boneless rolled pork loin roast	2 lb.

1. Combine soy sauce, sherry, honey, garlic and ginger in a glass loaf pan.
2. Place roast in sauce to marinate for several hours. Turn several times.
3. Drain roast and place on a microwavable roasting rack. Insert a microwavable meat thermometer or probe and cover with parchment or wax paper. Micro-cook on MEDIUM (70%) to 170°F
OR
Micro-cook on MEDIUM (70%) to 150°F. Replace the microwavable thermometer with a conventional thermometer and finish cooking on the barbecue until roast is 170°F.
4. Wrap roast in foil and let stand 15 minutes.

1 Serving	Calories	426	Carbohydrate	2 g
	Protein	31 g	Cholesterol	115 mg
	Fat	32 g	Sodium	343 mg

Pork Kabobs

Serves 4

6	carrots	6
500 g	lean boneless pork, cut in cubes	1 lb.
2	green peppers, cubed	2
1 recipe	Sweet Sour Sauce (page 192)	1 recipe

1. Peel carrots and cut into chunks. Place in a 1 L (1 qt.) microwavable casserole. Cover with water and soak for 10-15 minutes. Drain and micro-cook on HIGH (100%) for 4 minutes or until barely tender.
2. String cubes of pork on wooden skewers, alternating with carrots, pepper and pineapple tidbits from sauce. Baste with sauce.
3. Place on a microwavable rack and cover with wax or parchment paper. Micro-cook on HIGH (100%) for 8-10 minutes or until pork is cooked. Serve with sauce over cooked rice.

1 Serving	Calories	527	Carbohydrate	54 g
	Protein	25 g	Cholesterol	87 mg
	Fat	24 g	Sodium	170 mg

Savory Pork Ragout

Serves 4

2 slices	bacon, diced	2 slices
1	green pepper, diced	1
2	onions, sliced	2
250 g	mushrooms, sliced	8 oz.
2 mL	dried savory	1/2 tsp.
2 mL	dried oregano	1/2 tsp.
2 mL	salt	1/2 tsp.
few grinds	fresh black pepper	few grinds
1 can(540 mL)	tomatoes	1 can(19 oz.)
500 g	pork shoulder, cut in small cubes	1 lb.
50 mL	flour	1/4 cup
50 mL	water	1/4 cup

1. Place bacon in a 2.5 L (2 1/2 qt.) microwavable casserole and micro-cook on HIGH (100%) for 1 minute. Add green pepper, onions and mushrooms and micro-cook on HIGH (100%) for 5 minutes, stirring twice.
2. Add savory, oregano, salt, pepper and tomatoes. Blend well. Stir in meat, cover and micro-cook on HIGH (100%) for 5 minutes, then MEDIUM-LOW (50%) for 30 to 35 minutes or until meat is tender, stirring twice.
3. Mix flour and water and blend in. Micro-cook on HIGH (100%) for 1 minute until thickened.

1 Serving	Calories	366	Carbohydrate	19 g
	Protein	27 g	Cholesterol	90 mg
	Fat	20 g	Sodium	593 mg

Marmalade Ham

Serves 4

A fast main dish for a busy day.

4 slices	ready-to-eat ham	4 slices
50 mL	orange marmalade	1/4 cup
15 mL	orange juice or orange liqueur	1 Tbsp.
2 mL	dry mustard	1/2 tsp.
15 mL	brown sugar	1 Tbsp.

1. Arrange ham slices on a flat microwavable dish.
2. Combine remaining ingredients and spread over slices. Cover with parchment or wax paper.
3. Micro-cook on HIGH (100%) for 4 to 5 minutes or until hot.

1 Serving	Calories	230	Carbohydrate	18 g
	Protein	14 g	Cholesterol	33 mg
	Fat	11 g	Sodium	1030 mg

Creamy Ham Scallop

8 servings

This recipe serves 8 so plan to freeze half for a second meal.

1 kg	cooked ham	2 lb.
1 small	cauliflower	1 small
1 small bunch	broccoli	1 small bunch
4	carrots	4
4 stalks	celery	4 stalks
25 mL	butter	2 Tbsp.
15 mL	oil	1 Tbsp.
2	onions, sliced	2
2 cloves	garlic, minced	2 cloves
75 mL	flour	$1/3$ cup
few grinds	white pepper	few grinds
500 mL	chicken stock	2 cups
125 mL	milk	$1/2$ cup
250 mL	whole wheat cracker crumbs	1 cup
250 mL	grated Edam cheese	1 cup

1. Cut ham into bite-sized cubes.
2. Cut cauliflower and broccoli into florets. Cut carrots and celery into $1/2$ inch pieces. Weigh vegetables, place in a 3 L (3 qt.) microwavable casserole. Sprinkle with 5 mL (1 tsp.) water, cover and micro-cook on HIGH (100%) for 7 minutes per kg (5 minutes per pound) or until tender-crisp. Drain and set aside.
3. In a 750 mL (3 cup) microwavable container melt butter and oil on HIGH. Add onions and garlic and micro-cook on HIGH (100%) until onions are soft, stirring several times. Stir in flour and pepper. Gradually stir in stock and bring to a boil on HIGH (100%), stirring several times just before it reaches a boil. Stir once and bring to boil again. Blend in milk. Mix ham into vegetables and pour sauce over.
4. Combine crumbs and cheese and spread over top of casserole. Micro-cook on MEDIUM (70%) for 5 minutes or until heated through.
OR cook on Combination for 10 minutes.

Note: If not serving immediately after cooking, refrigerate after step 3. Reheat on MEDIUM (70%) until almost hot, then add topping and micro-cook on MEDIUM (70%) for 2 minutes.

1 Serving				
	Calories	440	Carbohydrate	18 g
	Protein	29 g	Cholesterol	70 mg
	Fat	28 g	Sodium	1622 mg

Veal Cordon Bleu

Serves 4

4 pieces	thin slices veal fillet	4 pieces
4	thin slices ham	4
4	thin slices Edam cheese	4
1	egg, beaten	1
75 mL	dry bread crumbs	1/3 cup
50 mL	oil	1/4 cup
	parsley for garnish	
	lemon slices for garnish	

1. Place veal between sheets of wax paper and flatten with mallet until thin, being careful not to tear meat.
2. Place a slice of ham and then cheese on top of each veal fillet. Roll up and seal ends. Secure with toothpicks if necessary. Dip each roll in beaten egg, and then in crumbs. Set aside.
3. Preheat a large browning dish for 6 minutes. Quickly add oil and carefully place veal rolls in the dish. Micro-cook on HIGH (100%) for 2 minutes. Turn rolls over and micro-cook on MEDIUM (70%) for 4-5 minutes. Drain on paper towels.
4. Place on serving dish and garnish with parsley and lemon slices.

1 Serving				
	Calories	402	Carbohydrate	7 g
	Protein	25 g	Cholesterol	156 mg
	Fat	30 g	Sodium	382 mg

Note: If a browning dish is not available place rolls in a shallow microwavable dish. Pour 50 mL (1/4 cup) butter in place of oil over rolls. Cover with parchment or wax paper and micro-cook on MEDIUM (70%) for 15 minutes or until cooked. They will not be as browned as with a browning dish.

Variation: Chicken Cordon Bleu
Use boneless half chicken breasts in place of the veal. If desired pour 50 mL (1/4 cup) white wine into browning dish to dissolve the browning from meat and pour over rolls.

Herbed Lamb Chops With Vegetables

Serves 4

A delicious, one dish meal using inexpensive, shoulder lamb chops.

3	carrots	3
150 g	fresh green beans	6 oz.
15 mL	oil	1 Tbsp.
4	shoulder lamb chops	4
2 cloves	garlic, minced	2 cloves
1	onion, chopped	1
125 mL	white wine	1/2 cup
15 mL	tomato paste	1 Tbsp.
125 mL	water	1/2 cup
1 pkg.	chicken bouillon	1 pkg.
2 mL	dried rosemary	1/2 tsp.
2 mL	thyme	1/2 tsp.
	salt and pepper	
30 mL	flour	2 Tbsp.
45 mL	water	3 Tbsp.
500 g	small new potatoes	1 lb.
12	fresh mushrooms	12

1. Cut carrots into 4 strips and then into 8 cm (3 in.) lengths. Soak carrots and green beans in water while preparing rest of dish.
2. Heat a large browning dish on HIGH (100%) for 6 minutes. Add oil and then brown lamb chops until sizzling stops. Add garlic, onion, wine, tomato paste, water, bouillon, rosemary, thyme and salt and pepper to taste. Cover and micro-cook on HIGH (100%) for 5 minutes then on MEDIUM (70%) for 5 minutes. Turn chops over.
3. Add carrots, beans and potatoes. Micro-cook on MEDIUM (70%) for 20 minutes.
4. Combine flour and water and stir into liquid in bottom of dish, mixing well. Add mushrooms. Micro-cook on LOW (30%) for 5 minutes. Let stand 5 minutes before serving.

1 Serving					
	Calories	471	Carbohydrate	33 g	
	Protein	24 g	Cholesterol	72 mg	
	Fat	28 g	Sodium	261 mg	

Herbed Lamb Chops
with
Potatoes • Green Beans • Carrots
Key Lime Pie

Herbed Lamb Chops with Vegetables (p. 68)
Florida Key Lime Pie (p. 138)

Seafood Stuffed Chicken Breasts

Serves 4

2	whole chicken breasts, halved, deboned and skinned	2
30 mL	butter	2 Tbsp.
75 mL	chopped green onion	1/3 cup
75 mL	chopped celery	1/3 cup
30 mL	dry white wine	2 Tbsp.
125 mL	seasoned stuffing mix	1/2 cup
1 can(150g)	crab, drained	1 can(5 oz.)
30 mL	butter	2 Tbsp.
30 mL	flour	2 Tbsp.
350 mL	light cream	1 1/3 cups
50 mL	grated Swiss cheese	1/4 cup
50 mL	dry white wine paprika	1/4 cup

1. Place chicken between sheets of wax paper and flatten with a mallet until they are about 0.5 cm (1/4" thick).
2. Place first amount of butter in a 750 mL (3 cup) microwavable container and micro-cook on HIGH (100%) about 30 seconds to melt. Add onion and celery and micro-cook on HIGH (100%) for 2 minutes or until tender. Add wine, stuffing and crab. Mix well.
3. Place 1/4 of the mixture on each breast and roll up tightly. Tie with string or hold with toothpicks. Place in a shallow microwavable baking dish and micro-cook, uncovered, on MEDIUM (70%) for 10 minutes or until chicken is cooked. Remove string or toothpicks.
4. Melt second amount of butter in a 750 mL (3 cup) microwavable container on HIGH (100%) and whisk in flour. Micro-cook cream on HIGH (100%) for 3 minutes. Blend into sauce and micro-cook on HIGH (100%) until mixture comes to a boil, stirring every 30 seconds. Add wine and cheese and stir to blend. Pour over chicken and garnish with paprika.

1 Serving				
	Calories	526	Carbohydrate	12 g
	Protein	40 g	Cholesterol	200 mg
	Fat	32 g	Sodium	421 mg

Chicken Rolls With Two Cheeses

Serves 4

2	whole chicken breasts, halved skinned and deboned	2
4	thin slices Swiss cheese	4
2	thin slices ham	2
2	green onions, finely chopped	2
5 mL	minced parsley	1 tsp.
1 small	clove garlic, minced	1 small
few grinds	black pepper	few grinds
25 mL	grated Parmesan cheese	2 Tbsp.
1	egg, beaten	1
50 mL	bread crumbs	1/4 cup
50 mL	oil	1/4 cup

1. Gently pound chicken between two sheets wax paper with a mallet until thin.
2. Top each piece with a slice of cheese and a half slice of ham.
3. Preheat a browning dish on HIGH (100%) according to manufacturer's directions.
4. Meanwhile combine green onions, parsley, garlic, pepper, Parmesan cheese and 5 mL (1 tsp.) of the beaten egg. Divide into 4 parts and form each into a log shape. Place at one end of chicken piece and roll up. Secure with toothpicks. Dip each roll into egg and then into crumbs.
5. When browning dish is hot add oil. Place chicken rolls in dish. Micro-cook on HIGH (100%) 1 minute. Turn rolls over and micro-cook on HIGH (100%) for 5 minutes longer. Remove toothpicks.

1 serving				
	Calories	474	Carbohydrate	7 g
	Protein	41 g	Cholesterol	181 mg
	Fat	30 g	Sodium	731 mg

Chicken Kiev

Serves 4

75 mL	butter, softened	1/3 cup
1	clove garlic, minced	1
	rind of 1/2 lemon	
25 mL	lemon juice	5 tsp.
15 mL	chopped fresh parsley	1 Tbsp.
50 mL	dry bread crumbs	1/4 cup
50 mL	Parmesan cheese	1/4 cup
2 mL	paprika	1/2 tsp.
2	whole boneless chicken breasts halved, skinned and deboned	2
	flour for dipping chicken	
1	egg, beaten	1
50 mL	oil	1/4 cup

1. Beat butter with garlic and lemon rind in a bowl. Gradually add lemon juice and parsley. Shape into a log about 20 cm (8 in.), wrap in wax paper and freeze until hard.
2. Mix bread crumbs, Parmesan and paprika together in a shallow dish.
3. Pound chicken breasts between sheets of wax paper or plastic wrap until about .5 cm (1/4 inch) thick.
4. Preheat a browning dish according to manufacturer's directions.
5. Meanwhile cut frozen butter log into 4 portions and place one on each breast. Tuck in sides and roll chicken breasts securing with toothpicks. Dip chicken in flour, then in beaten egg, and finally roll in bread crumb mixture.
6. When dish is hot, add oil and place rolls in pan. Micro-cook on HIGH (100%) for 1 minute. Turn and micro-cook on HIGH (100%) 4 minutes longer. Remove toothpicks.

1 Serving				
	Calories	518	Carbohydrate	10 g
	Protein	35 g	Cholesterol	200 mg
	Fat	37 g	Sodium	393 mg

Breaded Chicken Cutlets With Madeira

Serves 4

2	whole chickens breasts, halved, skinned and deboned	2
30 mL	butter	2 Tbsp.
15 mL	oil	1 Tbsp.
1	egg, beaten	1
175 mL	bread crumbs	3/4 cup
175 mL	grated Parmesan cheese	3/4 cup
1 mL	salt	1/4 tsp.
dash	pepper	dash
30 mL	butter	2 Tbsp.
50 mL	thinly sliced green onion	1/4 cup
125 mL	Madeira or sherry	1/2 cup

1. Cut each half chicken breast into 2 pieces.
2. Place first amount of butter in a shallow microwavable dish. Micro-cook on HIGH (100%) for 45 seconds to 1 minute, until melted. Stir in oil and egg until completely blended.
3. On a separate plate or on wax paper, combine bread crumbs, cheese, salt and pepper.
4. Dip each piece of chicken into butter-egg mixture and then into crumb mixture, pressing coating into place with hands.
5. Arrange chicken pieces with thicker sections towards the outside of a shallow microwavable dish. Cover with parchment or wax paper and micro-cook on HIGH (100%) for 5 minutes. Turn over and micro-cook on MEDIUM (70%) for 3 to 5 minutes more, or until meat tests done. Remove chicken to a serving platter and cover to keep warm.
6. Add second amount of butter and green onions to cooking dish. Micro-cook on HIGH (100%) for 1 minute. Stir in wine and continue cooking on HIGH (100%) for 3 minutes, stirring once.
7. Return chicken to dish with the wine sauce. Cover with wax paper and micro-cook on HIGH (100%) 2 minutes or until heated through. Serve immediately.

1 Serving	Calories	468	Carbohydrate	17 g
	Protein	40 g	Cholesterol	198 mg
	Fat	26 g	Sodium	679 mg

Herbed Chicken Breasts and Peas With Rice

Serves 4

250 mL	long grain converted rice	1 cup
500 mL	hot water	2 cups
5 mL	salt	1 tsp.
4 slices	bacon	4 slices
2	whole chicken breasts, halved and skinned	2
125 mL	chopped onion	1/2 cup
1 clove	garlic, minced	1 clove
25mL	dry white wine	2 Tbsp.
2 mL	basil	1/2 tsp.
2 mL	oregano	1/2 tsp.
1 mL	salt	1/4 tsp.
1 pkg.(280g)	frozen peas	1 pkg. (10 oz.)
2	tomatoes, cut in wedges	2
25 mL	chopped parsley	2 Tbsp.

1. Combine rice, hot water and salt in a 2.5 L (2 1/2 qt.) microwavable container. Cover and micro-cook on HIGH (100%) for 5 minutes or until boiling. Micro-cook on LOW (30%) for 8 minutes. Let stand while preparing chicken.
2. Cut bacon in 2 cm (1/2 inch) pieces. Place in a 2 L (2 qt.) microwavable casserole. Micro-cook on HIGH (100%) for 4 minutes or until crisp. Remove and set aside.
3. Turn chicken breasts in bacon grease to coat and arrange skin side down. Cover with parchment or wax paper and micro-cook on HIGH (100%) for 5 minutes.
4. Combine onion, garlic, wine, herbs and salt. Turn chicken pieces over and pour onion mixture over top. Cover and micro-cook on MEDIUM (70%) for 5 minutes.
5. Add peas, cover and micro-cook on HIGH (100%) for 5 minutes.
6. Add tomato wedges, parsley and reserved bacon. Cover and micro-cook on HIGH (100%) for 3 to 5 minutes or until chicken is done and peas are heated through.
Serve with rice.

1 Serving				
	Calories	514	Carbohydrate	52 g
	Protein	38 g	Cholesterol	92 mg
	Fat	16 g	Sodium	877 mg

Chicken Oriental

Serves 4

2	whole chicken breasts, skinned and deboned	2
150 g	snow peas	6 oz.
100 g	fresh mushrooms	4 oz.
3-4	green onions	3-4
125 mL	water chestnuts	$1/2$ cup
50 mL	water	$1/4$ cup
50 mL	light soy sauce	$1/4$ cup
30 mL	cornstarch	2 Tbsp.

1. Cut chicken into thin slices. Place in a 1.5 L (6 cup) microwavable container. Cover and micro-cook on HIGH (100%) for 5 to 6 minutes or until chicken is opaque and tender, stirring after 3 minutes.
2. While chicken cooks, snap ends and remove strings from snow peas. Slice mushrooms, green onions and water chestnuts.
3. Add vegetables to chicken, cover and micro-cook on HIGH (100%) for 2 minutes.
4. While chicken is cooking combine water, soy sauce and cornstarch. Stir into chicken and micro-cook on HIGH (100%) for 3 minutes or until sauce has thickened, stirring after 2 minutes.

1 Serving	Calories	230	Carbohydrate	15 g
	Protein	34 g	Cholesterol	77 mg
	Fat	4 g	Sodium	1171 mg

Hawaiian Chicken

Serves 4

2	whole chicken breasts, halved and skinned	2
15 mL	oil	1 Tbsp.
1 can(398 mL)	pineapple tidbits	1 can(14 oz.)
50 mL	brown sugar	1/4 cup
0.5 mL	ginger	1/8 tsp.
25 mL	cornstarch	2 Tbsp.
5 mL	soy sauce	1 tsp.
30 mL	cider vinegar	2 Tbsp.

1. Preheat a large browning dish on HIGH (100%) for 6 minutes. Add oil. Place chicken breasts in dish meat side down. Micro-cook on HIGH (100%) for 1 minute. Remove from oven and set aside.
2. Drain juice from pineapple into a 750 mL/3 cup microwavable container. Add enough water to make 175 mL (3/4 cup) liquid. Stir in sugar, ginger, cornstarch and soy sauce. Bring to a boil on HIGH (100%) power, stirring twice. Stir in vinegar.
3. Pour sauce over chicken. Cover and micro-cook on MEDIUM (70%) for 10 minutes. Stir in pineapple. Let stand 5 minutes and serve over rice.

1 Serving					
	Calories	322	Carbohydrate	36 g
	Protein	30 g	Cholesterol	77 mg
	Fat	7 g	Sodium	144 mg

Chicken a l'orange

Serves 4

4	chicken pieces(legs and thighs or ½ breasts), skinned	4
few grinds	fresh pepper	few grinds
30 mL	sherry	2 Tbsp.
15 mL	butter	1 Tbsp.
3	green onions, sliced	3
125 mL	orange juice	½ cup
30 mL	orange marmalade	2 Tbsp.
20 mL	cornstarch	1 Tbsp. + 1 tsp.
1	orange	1

1. Arrange chicken in a shallow microwavable dish. Sprinkle with pepper and sherry. Cover with parchment or wax paper and micro-cook on MEDIUM (70%) for 8 minutes. Turn pieces over and micro-cook at MEDIUM (70%) another 6 to 8 minutes or until chicken is tender. Pour off cooking liquid and reserve.
2. In a 750 mL (3 cup) microwavable container micro-cook butter on HIGH (100%) until melted. Add onions and micro-cook on HIGH (100%) for 1 minute or until onions are soft.
3. Blend in orange juice, marmalade, reserved cooking liquid and cornstarch. Micro-cook on HIGH (100%) about 2 to 3 minutes or until boiling and thickened, stirring several times.
4. Pour sauce over chicken and garnish with orange sections.

1 Serving	Calories	274	Carbohydrate	16 g
	Protein	26 g	Cholesterol	98 mg
	Fat	11 g	Sodium	118 mg

Saucy Barbecued Chicken

Serves 4

1	frying chicken, cut up	1
250 mL	Barbecue Sauce (p. 193)	1 cup

1. Arrange chicken in a shallow microwavable dish. Pour sauce over. Cover with parchment or wax paper. Micro-cook on MEDIUM (70%) for 18 minutes per kg or 8 minutes per pound [approximately 25 minutes for 1.5 kg (3 lb.) chicken].

Note: This is delicious cooked on the Combination program. Use the program for chicken as directed for your oven.

1 Serving	Calories	451	Carbohydrate	12 g
	Protein	46 g	Cholesterol	157 mg
	Fat	24 g	Sodium	770 mg

Golden Glazed Chicken

Serves 4

4 pieces	chicken, (legs & thighs or 1/2 breasts)	4 pieces
50 mL	honey	1/4 cup
15 mL	butter	1 Tbsp.
45 mL	Dijon-type mustard	3 Tbsp.
2 mL	curry powder	1/2 tsp.
2 mL	garlic salt	1/2 tsp.
2 mL	lemon juice	1/2 tsp.

1. Arrange chicken in a single layer in a shallow microwavable baking dish.
2. Combine remaining ingredients and pour over chicken. Cover with parchment or wax paper and micro-cook on HIGH (100%) for 10 minutes and then on LOW (30%) for 20 minutes. Baste several times.

1 Serving				
	Calories	263	Carbohydrate	13 g
	Protein	26 g	Cholesterol	98 mg
	Fat	12 g	Sodium	494 mg

Crusty Fried Chicken

Serves 4

250 mL	finely crushed cornflakes or bread crumbs	1 cup
30 mL	dried parsley flakes	2 Tbsp.
3 mL	salt	3/4 tsp.
1 mL	oregano	1/4 tsp.
dash	pepper	1/8 tsp.
25 mL	grated Parmesan cheese	2 Tbsp.
50 mL	butter, melted	1/4 cup
1	frying chicken, quartered	1

1. Combine crumbs, parsley, salt, oregano and pepper in a flat bowl.
2. Place butter in a flat bowl. Dip chicken pieces in butter and then in crumb mixture.
3. Place chicken on a microwavable rack. Place a piece of parchment or wax paper over top. Micro-cook on MEDIUM (70%) 25 to 30 minutes (18 minutes per kg or 8 minutes per pound of chicken) or until juices run clear.

Note: Prepackaged coating mix may be used in place of butter and crumb mixture. Just moisten the chicken and shake as directed.

1 Serving				
	Calories	565	Carbohydrate	12 g
	Protein	47 g	Cholesterol	192 mg
	Fat	36 g	Sodium	793 mg

Poulet Chasseur (Hunter's Chicken)

Serves 4

The delicious combination of flavours in this traditional dish is easy to achieve in your microwave.

1	frying chicken, cut up	1
125 mL	flour	1/2 cup
25 mL	butter	2 Tbsp.
3	dry shallots (or 1 small onion) chopped	3
1	small clove garlic, minced	1
25 mL	butter	2 Tbsp.
250 mL	sliced fresh mushrooms	1 cup
50 mL	tomato sauce	1/4 cup
15 mL	chopped parsley	1 Tbsp.
5 mL	thyme	1 tsp.
2	bay leaves	2
1 mL	freshly ground black pepper	1/4 tsp.
2 mL	salt	1/2 tsp.
5 mL	beef bouillon granules	1 tsp.
125 mL	dry white wine	1/2 cup
15 mL	brandy	1 Tbsp.
	parsley for garnish	

1. Preheat a large browning dish for 6 minutes. Meanwhile skin chicken and dust with flour.
2. When dish is hot add first amount of butter and then chicken pieces. After a few seconds turn over and micro-cook on HIGH (100%) for 2 minutes. Remove from oven, cover and let stand.
3. In a 750 mL (3 cup) microwavable container place shallots, garlic and second amount of butter. Micro-cook on HIGH (100%) for 3 minutes until the onion is lightly browned. Stir in mushrooms and micro-cook on HIGH (100%) for 4 minutes.
4. Stir in tomato sauce, herbs, pepper, salt, bouillon granules, wine and brandy. Micro-cook on HIGH (100%) for 3 minutes.
5. Pour sauce over chicken, cover with lid and micro-cook on LOW (30%) for 20 minutes. Remove bay leaves and garnish with parsley.

1 Serving					
	Calories	444	Carbohydrate	18 g	
	Protein	44 g	Cholesterol	158 mg	
	Fat	21 g	Sodium	730 mg	

Chicken and Dumplings

Serves 4

1	frying chicken, cut up	1
250 mL	chicken broth	1 cup
1	onion, quartered	1
2 sprigs	fresh parsley	2 sprigs
1	bay leaf	1
15 mL	flour	1 Tbsp.
15 mL	water	1 Tbsp.

1. Place chicken, broth, onion, parsley and bay leaf in a 2 L (2 qt.) microwavable baking dish. Micro-cook on HIGH (100%) for 10-12 minutes or until boiling, then on LOW (30%) for 20 minutes. Remove chicken from liquid and let cool.
2. Strain broth and return to pan. Remove meat from bones and return to pan. Combine flour and water and stir in. Micro-cook on HIGH (100%) about 2 minutes until boiling and thickened, stirring once. Make dumplings.

1 Serving	Calories	316	Carbohydrate	7 g
	Protein	44 g	Cholesterol	126 mg
	Fat	11 g	Sodium	155 mg

Dumplings:

375 mL	all-purpose flour	1 1/2 cups
2 mL	dried parsley	1/2 tsp.
2 mL	dried savory	1/2 tsp.
2 mL	salt	1/2 tsp.
10 mL	baking powder	2 tsp.
175 mL	milk	3/4 cup
1	egg	1
30 mL	oil	2 Tbsp.

1. Combine flour, parsley, savory, salt and baking powder.
2. Combine milk, egg and oil, mixing well.
3. Stir milk mixture into flour mixture and stir lightly with a fork just to combine. Drop over boiling chicken broth. Cover and micro-cook on HIGH (100%) for 5 minutes or until just set.

1 Serving	Calories	307	Carbohydrate	48 g
	Protein	7 g	Cholesterol	75 mg
	Fat	10 g	Sodium	270 mg

Stuffed Turkey Breast

Serves 4

140 g	fresh spinach	10 oz.
50 mL	grated Parmesan cheese	1/4 cup
15 mL	chopped shallots	1 Tbsp.
1	small clove garlic, minced	1
1/2	boneless turkey breast	1/2
1	egg white	1
25 mL	dry Italian bread crumbs	2 Tbsp.
2 mL	paprika	1/2 tsp.

1. Wash and stem spinach and place in a 1 L (1 qt.) microwavable container along with shallots and garlic. Cover and micro-cook on HIGH (100%) for 3 to 4 minutes or just until spinach is wilted. Blend in cheese.
2. Cut a pocket in the turkey breast and spoon spinach mixture into opening. Secure openings with toothpicks. Place on a microwavable rack, and brush with beaten egg white. Combine bread crumbs and paprika in a small dish and sprinkle over top. Cover with parchment or wax paper.
3. Micro-cook on MEDIUM (70%) for 22 minutes per kg (10 minutes per pound). Let stand 10 minutes before slicing.

1 Serving				
	Calories	179	Carbohydrate	5 g
	Protein	3? g	Cholesterol	81 mg
	Fat	3 g	Sodium	213 mg

Cornish Game Hens With Crab Stuffing

Serves 4

25 mL	butter	2 Tbsp.
25 mL	chopped shallots or onion	2 Tbsp.
25 mL	chopped green pepper	2 Tbsp.
1 can(127 g)	crab meat, drained	1 can (4.5 oz.)
4 slices	firm bread, broken into small bits	4 slices
5 mL	chopped parsley	1 tsp.
4	Cornish Game Hens	4
25 mL	dark soy sauce	2 Tbsp.
75 mL	water	1/3 cup
5 mL	cornstarch	1 tsp.

1. Make crab stuffing: Melt butter in a 750 mL (3 cup) microwavable container on HIGH. Add shallots and micro-cook on HIGH (100%) 1 minute. Combine green pepper, crab, bread crumbs and parsley. Use to stuff the 4 Cornish hens.

2. Make glaze: Combine soy sauce, water and cornstarch in a small microwavable container and micro-cook on HIGH (100%) for 1 to 2 minutes or until boiling. Stir once. Brush over hens to glaze. Place hens breast side down on a roasting rack and cover with parchment or wax paper. Estimate cooking time at 20 to 22 minutes per kg (9 to 10 minutes per pound) and micro-cook on MEDIUM (70%) for half the time. Turn hens over, brush again with glaze and cook for remaining time or until legs move freely.

1 Serving					
	Calories	576	Carbohydrate	14 g	
	Protein	68 g	Cholesterol	235 mg	
	Fat	26 g	Sodium	918 mg	

Grilled Salmon

Serves 4

If you want a special treat, grill salmon in your microwave.

4	salmon steaks about 150 g or 5 oz. each	4
15 mL	lemon juice	1 Tbsp.
	salt	
	freshly ground pepper	
25 mL	flour	2 Tbsp.
25 mL	butter	2 Tbsp.
	lemon slices to garnish	

1. Preheat a large browning dish on HIGH (100%) for 6 minutes. Meanwhile rinse and dry salmon steaks. Sprinkle with lemon juice and coat with flour mixed with salt and pepper.
2. When dish is hot, add butter and quickly put in steaks, arranging them so that the thickest parts are towards the outside of the dish, pressing steaks to pan. Micro-cook on HIGH (100%) for 3 minutes. Turn steaks over and micro-cook on HIGH (100%) for another 3 minutes or until the fish flakes easily.
3. Cover and allow to stand 5 minutes. Garnish with slices of lemon before serving.

Note: If you do not have a browning dish, place salmon steaks on a shallow microwavable dish. Brush with melted butter. Cover with parchment or wax paper. Micro-cook on HIGH (100%) for 8 to 9 minutes or until fish flakes easily.

1 Serving				
	Calories	302	Carbohydrate	3 g
	Protein	35 g	Cholesterol	76 mg
	Fat	16 g	Sodium	207 mg

Salmon and Pasta With Vegetables

Serves 4

A delicious, one dish medley of salmon and vegetables with a Swiss cheese sauce.

175 mL	carrots, sliced 6 mm (¹/₄in.)thick	³/₄ cup
1 small bunch	broccoli, cut into small florets	1 small bunch
200 g	fettuccine noodles	7 oz.
1 clove	garlic, minced	1 clove
250 mL	mushrooms, sliced thickly	1 cup
3	green onions, cut into 2.5 cm (1 inch) pieces	3
¹/₂	small onion, minced	¹/₂
25 mL	butter	2 Tbsp.
25 mL	all-purpose flour	2 Tbsp.
1 mL	salt	¹/₄ tsp.
	few grindings white pepper	
425 mL	milk	1 ³/₄ cups
1	chicken bouillon cube or packet	1
125 mL	grated Swiss cheese	¹/₂ cup
50 mL	Parmesan cheese	¹/₄ cup
2 cans(213 g)	salmon, drained	2 cans(7.5 oz.)

1. Soak carrots in cold water while preparing other vegetables. Wash broccoli and shake slightly.
2. Cook fettuccine noodles: Place 1.5 L (6 cups) water in a 3 L (3 qt.) microwavable container. Add about 5 mL (1 tsp.) salt and bring to a boil on HIGH. Stir in noodles; cover and micro-cook on HIGH (100%) for 6 to 8 minutes or until just tender. Drain, rinse in hot water and set aside. [If desired, cook noodles on the stove while preparing vegetables and sauce in your microwave.]
3. In a 2.5 L (2.5 qt.) microwavable casserole combine carrots, broccoli, garlic, mushrooms, and onions. Cover and micro-cook on HIGH (100%) for 8 to 10 minutes or until vegetables are tender. Stir several times. Let stand, covered. Drain.
4. Place butter in a 750 mL (3 cup) microwavable container and micro-cook on HIGH (100%) for 30 seconds. Stir in flour and seasonings. Micro-cook milk on HIGH (100%) for 4 minutes or until hot but not boiling. Gradually whisk milk into flour mixture and add bouillon cube. Micro-cook on HIGH (100%), stirring every 30 seconds until mixture comes to a boil and is thickened. Stir in cheeses.
5. Flake salmon, removing bones if desired. Stir into vegetable mixture and then blend in cheese sauce. Finally add noodles. Reheat on MEDIUM (70%) if needed before serving. Sprinkle with more Parmesan if desired.

1 Serving	Calories	674	Carbohydrate	61 g
	Protein	40 g	Cholesterol	75 mg
	Fat	30 g	Sodium	1165 mg

Salmon Cups With Parsley Sauce

Serves 4

A good recipe for a day when you haven't shopped for groceries. Extra salmon cups freeze very well.

10 mL	butter	2 tsp.
4	green onions, sliced	4
2 cans(213 g)	salmon, red or pink	2 cans(7.5 oz.)
125 mL	crackers, crushed (12 crackers)	1/2 cup
1	egg	1
1	egg white	1
50 mL	milk	1/4 cup

1. Combine butter and onions in a small microwavable container. Micro-cook on HIGH (100%) for 1 minute.
2. Drain salmon and remove bones if desired. Add onions and crackers.
3. Beat egg, egg white and milk together and blend with salmon mixture.
4. Divide mixture among 4 (170 mL or 4 oz.) custard dishes.
5. Micro-cook on HIGH (100%) for 4 to 5 minutes or until set. Allow to stand for 5 minutes and turn out onto serving plate.

Parsley Sauce

50 mL	butter	1/4 cup
1	egg yolk	1
15 mL	lemon juice	1 Tbsp.
1 mL	dry mustard	1/4 tsp.
dash	salt	dash
25 mL	mayonnaise	2 Tbsp.
5 mL	chopped fresh parsley	1 tsp.

1. Place butter in a small microwavable container. Micro-cook on HIGH (100%) for 45 seconds.
2. Blend egg yolk, lemon juice, mustard and salt into butter. Micro-cook on MEDIUM (70%) for 10 seconds, stir and micro-cook 5 seconds longer on MEDIUM (70%). Whisk vigorously. Micro-cook an additional 5 seconds if necessary. Be sure not to overcook or mixture will curdle. (It should be the consistency of thick cream.)
3. Stir in mayonnaise and parsley and spoon over salmon.

1 Serving				
	Calories	493	Carbohydrate	9 g
	Protein	26 g	Cholesterol	231 mg
	Fat	39 g	Sodium	726 mg

Fish Rings Florentine

Serves 4

500 g	sole fillets	1 lb.
250 mL	fresh bread crumbs (about 3 slices)	1 cup
500 mL	fresh spinach leaves, washed and trimmed	2 cups
250 mL	sliced fresh mushrooms	1 cup
30 mL	chopped onion	2 Tbsp.
1	egg	1
30 mL	grated Parmesan cheese	2 Tbsp.
2 mL	salt	$1/2$ tsp.
few grinds	pepper	few grinds
$1/2$	lemon	$1/2$

1. Cut fish fillets in pieces 13 to 15 cm (5 to 6 inches) in length and about 1 cm ($1/3$ inch) thick. Curl each piece into a circle, overlapping ends. Fasten with toothpicks. Arrange on a shallow microwavable baking dish.

2. In a food processor make bread crumbs. Remove and set aside. Place spinach, mushrooms, onion, egg, cheese, salt and pepper in processor and pulse until finely chopped. Stir in bread crumbs.

3. Spoon spinach mixture into centre of fish rings. Cover with lid, parchment or wax paper and micro-cook on HIGH (100%) for 5 to 6 minutes or until fish is cooked. Let stand 3 minutes.

4. Cut lemon into slices or wedges and serve with sole.

1 Serving				
	Calories	339	Carbohydrate	23 g
	Protein	35 g	Cholesterol	159 mg
	Fat	11 g	Sodium	736 mg

Blackened Fish Fillets

Serves 4

A super easy fish dish in the popular Cajun tradition.

500 g	fish fillets	1 lb.
45 mL	melted butter	3 Tbsp.
15 mL	paprika	1 Tbsp.
2 mL	garlic salt	1/2 tsp.
10 mL	ground black pepper	2 tsp.
1 mL	cayenne pepper	1/4 tsp.
2 mL	oregano	1/2 tsp.
1 mL	thyme	1/4 tsp.

1. Arrange fish in a single layer on a shallow microwavable serving dish. Pour butter over.
2. Mix spices and sprinkle as much over fish as desired (reserve any remaining spices for another time). Cover with wax or parchment paper and micro-cook on HIGH (100%) for 6 minutes or until fish flakes easily. Let stand 3 minutes.

1 Serving	Calories	293	Carbohydrate	6 g
	Protein	28 g	Cholesterol	106 mg
	Fat	18 g	Sodium	542 mg

Super Sole

Serves 4

Easy, quick and tasty.

500 g	sole filets	1 lb.
75 mL	mayonnaise	1/3 cup
5 mL	lemon juice	1 tsp.
1	green onion, chopped	1
	grated Parmesan or Romano cheese	

1. Place sole cut side up on a shallow microwavable baking dish in a single layer.
2. Combine mayonnaise, lemon juice and onion and spread thinly over fish pieces. Sprinkle with cheese.
3. Cover with parchment or wax paper and micro-cook on HIGH (100%) for 6 minutes or until fish flakes easily. Let stand 3 minutes. Serve with wedges of lemon or lime.

1 Serving	Calories	332	Carbohydrate	1 g
	Protein	28 g	Cholesterol	116 mg
	Fat	24 g	Sodium	354 mg

Fish Vegetable Scallop

Serves 4

A tasty way to serve fish, even if fish isn't your favourite food.

3 strips	bacon, diced	3 strips
1 medium	onion	1 medium
1/2	green pepper, chopped	1/2
1 stalk	celery	1 stalk
30 mL	chopped fresh parsley	2 Tbsp.
4	mushrooms, sliced	4
25 mL	flour	2 Tbsp.
175 mL	milk	3/4 cup
2 mL	salt	1/2 tsp.
500 g	fish fillets, defrosted	1 lb.
75 mL	grated Cheddar cheese	1/3 cup

1. Place bacon in a 1 L (1 qt.) microwavable container. Micro-cook on HIGH (100%) for 2 minutes. Stir in onion, green pepper, celery, parsley and mushrooms and micro-cook about 2 minutes or until vegetables are tender.
2. Stir in flour, then blend in milk and salt. Micro-cook on HIGH (100%) for 3 minutes or until mixture comes to a boil, stirring several times.
3. Place fish in a shallow microwavable baking dish.
4. Pour sauce over fish. Cover with wax or parchment paper and micro-cook on HIGH (100%) for 5 to 6 minutes. Sprinkle with cheese and allow to stand 5 minutes.

1 Serving				
	Calories	377	Carbohydrate	10 g
	Protein	34 g	Cholesterol	107 mg
	Fat	22 g	Sodium	665 mg

Spaghetti With Clam Sauce

Serves 4

15 mL	oil	1 Tbsp.
2	garlic cloves, minced	2
1 small	onion, chopped	1 small
1 can(284 mL)	stewed tomatoes	1 can(10 oz.)
1 can(213 mL)	tomato sauce	1 can(7.5 oz.)
5 mL	dried basil	1 tsp.
5 mL	dried parsley	1 tsp.
0.5 mL	black pepper	1/8 tsp.
1 can(280 mL)	clams, drained	1 can(10 oz.)
375 g	spaghetti	12 oz.

1. In a 1.5 L (6 cup) microwavable casserole with lid, combine oil, garlic and onion. Cover and micro-cook on HIGH (100%) for 1 to 2 minutes or until onion is slightly tender.

2. Add tomatoes, sauce, basil, parsley, and pepper to onion mixture. Micro-cook on HIGH (100%) for 5 minutes, stirring once. Add clams. Micro-cook on HIGH (100%) for 2 to 3 minutes or until hot, stirring once.

3. Cook spaghetti until "al dente": Place 1.5 L (6 cups) water in a 3 L (3 qt.) microwavable container. Add about 5 mL (1 tsp.) salt and bring to a boil on HIGH (100%). Add spaghetti , cover and micro-cook on HIGH (100%) for 6 to 8 minutes or just until tender. Let stand 5 minutes. Meanwhile reheat sauce if necessary. [Cook spaghetti conventionally if desired while cooking sauce.]

4. Drain spaghetti and place in a serving bowl. Pour sauce over and toss well.

1 Serving				
	Calories	439	Carbohydrate	70 g
	Protein	23 g	Cholesterol	44 mg
	Fat	7 g	Sodium	217 mg

Tuna With Green Beans and Rice

Serves 4

A meal in a dish that's popular with all ages.

125 g	cream cheese	4 oz.
1 can(284 mL)	cream of mushroom soup	1 can(10 oz.)
500 mL	cooked rice	2 cups
1 can(182 mL)	tuna, drained	1 can(6.5 oz.)
1 pkg.(300 g)	frozen French-style green beans, defrosted	1 pkg.(10.5 oz.)
1	onion, chopped	1
15 mL	chopped fresh parsley	1 Tbsp.
dash	pepper	dash
50 mL	Parmesan cheese	1/4 cup
	paprika	

1. Soften cream cheese in a 2 L (2qt.) microwavable casserole on HIGH (100%) for 20 to 30 seconds. Blend in soup.
2. Stir in rice, tuna, beans, onion, parsley and pepper. Micro-cook on HIGH (100%) for 5 minutes. Stir well.
3. Sprinkle with cheese and paprika. Cover and micro-cook on MEDIUM (70%) for 10 minutes or until heated through.

1 Serving				
	Calories	507	Carbohydrate	40 g
	Protein	23 g	Cholesterol	66 mg
	Fat	29 g	Sodium	2213 mg

◇ *To tell if a casserole is heated to the centre, place your hand on the bottom. If it feels hot, the casserole is heated through.*

Tuna Salad Pita Pockets

Serves 6

A different idea for a tasty lunch.

250 mL	drained crushed pineapple	1 cup
15 mL	pineapple juice	1 Tbsp.
1 can(196 mL)	tuna	1 can(7 oz.)
250 mL	shredded cabbage	1 cup
30 mL	chopped pimento-stuffed olives	2 Tbsp.
50 mL	mayonnaise	1/4 cup
1 mL	celery salt	1/4 tsp.
dash	pepper	dash
6	pita, cut in quarters	6

1. Combine all ingredients except pita. Spoon into pita pockets. Arrange in a circle on a microwavable rack. Micro-cook on HIGH (100%) 2 to 3 minutes or until hot.

1 serving	Calories	288	Carbohydrate	32 g
	Protein	13 g	Cholesterol	37 mg
	Fat	12 g	Sodium	719 mg

◇ *For a tasty hot sandwich, layer sliced cold meat and cheese in a bun spread with butter and/or mayonnaise. Wrap in a white paper towel and micro-cook on MEDIUM (70%) for 30 to 60 seconds or until sandwich is warm.*

Spanish Eggs

Serves 4

30 mL	olive oil	2 Tbsp.
100 g	spicy sausage	4 oz.
125 mL	chopped onion	1/2 cup
1 clove	garlic, minced	1 clove
1	green or red pepper	1
250 mL	canned tomatoes	1 cup
5 mL	dried parsley	1 tsp.
1	small bay leaf	1
4	eggs	4

1. Heat a large browning skillet on HIGH (100%) for 6 minutes. Add oil and sausage and brown in skillet, stirring to crumble. Add onion, garlic and peppers and micro-cook on HIGH (100%), uncovered, for 2 minutes.
2. Add tomatoes and spices and micro-cook on HIGH (100%) for 5 minutes.
3. Drop eggs into hot sauce. Cover and micro-cook on MEDIUM (70%) about 2 minutes or until eggs are set to desired doneness. Let stand 2 to 3 minutes.

1 Serving	Calories	302	Carbohydrate	7 g
	Protein	11 g	Cholesterol	321 mg
	Fat	26 g	Sodium	351 mg

◇ *Eggs are very sensitive to microwave energy so be careful not to overcook them or they will be rubbery. Check for doneness before the expected time has elapsed and add more time if necessary.*

Swiss Breakfast Pie

23 cm (9 inch) pie

6 slices	bacon, diced	6 slices
250 mL	frozen hash brown or diced french fry potatoes	1 cup
1 mL	seasoned salt	1/4 tsp.
50 mL	chopped green onions	1/4 cup
125 mL	sliced mushrooms	1/2 cup
250 mL	grated Swiss cheese	1 cup
	salt and pepper	
3	eggs	3
50 mL	sour cream, milk or yogurt	1/4 cup

1. Place bacon in a small microwavable container. Micro-cook on HIGH (100%) about 6 minutes or until crisp, stirring twice.
2. Spread frozen potatoes into a greased, deep 23 cm (9 inch) glass pie plate. Micro-cook on HIGH (100%) for 1 1/2 minutes. Sprinkle with seasoned salt.
3. Layer onions, mushrooms, bacon and cheese evenly over potatoes. Sprinkle with salt and pepper.
4. Combine eggs and sour cream and pour over layers. Cover with wax or parchment paper and micro-cook on MEDIUM (70%) for 10 minutes or until set.

1 Serving — 1/6 of pie	Calories	240	Carbohydrate	8 g
	Protein	12 g	Cholesterol	185 mg
	Fat	18 g	Sodium	397 mg

Eggs Benedict

Serves 4

1 recipe	Hollandaise Sauce (page 190)	1 recipe
2	English muffins	2
4	slices ham	4
4	eggs	4

1. Prepare Hollandaise Sauce.
2. Cut muffins in two and toast.
3. Place ham on microwavable platter and micro-cook on HIGH (100%) 1 minute or until hot.
4. Bring 250 mL (1 cup) water to a boil in a 2 L (2 qt.) microwavable plastic cake pan or ring mould. (Glass cookware will not give a well-cooked egg.) Drop eggs into water, cover and micro-cook on MEDIUM (70%) for 2 minutes or until cooked to desired doneness. Let stand 30 seconds and remove from water with slotted spoon.
5. Place a slice of ham on each muffin, top with eggs and nap with sauce.

1 Serving	Calories	453	Carbohydrate	13 g
	Protein	15 g	Cholesterol	515 mg
	Fat	38 g	Sodium	896 mg

California Quiche

25 cm (10 inch) pie

1	baked 25 cm (10inch) pie or quiche shell	1
500 mL	Monterey Jack cheese, grated	2 cups
6 strips	bacon, cooked and crumbled	6 strips
50 mL	chopped green pepper	1/4 cup
3	green onions, sliced	3
125 mL	small shrimp	1/2 cup
1 can(364 mL)	evaporated milk	1 can(13 oz.)
4	eggs	4

1. Layer cheese, bacon, green pepper, onion and shrimp in bottom of baked pie shell.
2. Micro-cook milk on HIGH (100%) for 2 minutes. Beat eggs and add milk, beating well. Pour over cheese mixture and cover with parchment or wax paper. Elevate pie on a microwavable rack and micro-cook on MEDIUM (70%) for 12 minutes or until set. Let stand 5 minutes before serving.

Note: If you have a Combination oven bake pie shell in preheated oven at 450°F for 8 to 10 minutes. Finish preparing quiche and micro-cook as directed. There is no need to wait until oven is cool.

1 Serving — 1/8 of pie	Calories	379	Carbohydrate	16 g
	Protein	20 g	Cholesterol	218 mg
	Fat	26 g		

Quick Sausage Mushroom "Quiche"

23 cm (9 inch) pie

This quiche forms its own crust.

225 g	frozen spicy sausage meat	8 oz.
250 mL	sliced fresh mushrooms	1 cup
125 mL	chopped onions	1/2 cup
250 mL	grated Cheese — Swiss, Cheddar, Monterey Jack	1 cup
4	eggs	4
250 mL	milk	1 cup
75 mL	flour	1/3 cup
2 mL	dry mustard	1/2 tsp.
2 mL	salt	1/2 tsp.

1. Place frozen sausage meat in a deep 23 cm (9 inch) glass pie plate. Micro-cook on MEDIUM (70%) for 3 minutes. Chop into small pieces. Micro-cook on HIGH (100%) for 3 minutes longer or until no longer pink.
2. Stir in mushrooms and onions and micro-cook on HIGH (100%) for 2 minutes. Drain. Sprinkle top with grated cheese.
3. Combine eggs, milk, flour, mustard and salt, mixing thoroughly. Pour over sausage mixture. Cover with wax or parchment paper. Micro-cook on MEDIUM (70%) for 8 to 10 minutes or until set. Let stand 10 minutes before serving.

1 Serving — 1/6 of pie				
	Calories	347	Carbohydrate	10 g
	Protein	16 g	Cholesterol	249 mg
	Fat	27 g	Sodium	592 mg

Pizza Strata

Serves 6

A good dish to serve for Sunday night supper or have prepared and ready to cook after skiing.

8 slices	white bread	8 slices
15 mL	butter	1 Tbsp.
1	green pepper, sliced	1
1	onion, sliced	1
85 g	sliced pepperoni	3 oz.
250 g	Mozzarella cheese, grated	8 oz.
4	eggs	4
2 mL	oregano	1/2 tsp.
2 mL	salt	1/2 tsp.
500 mL	milk	2 cups

1. Cube bread and place in a 20 cm (8 inch) microwavable round or square pan.
2. In a small microwavable container, micro-cook butter, peppers, and onions on HIGH (100%) for 2 minutes or until onions are soft. Spread evenly over bread cubes. Layer pepperoni over top of vegetables and sprinkle with grated cheese.
3. Combine eggs, oregano, salt and milk. Pour over bread mixture. Cover with plastic wrap and let stand in refrigerator several hours or overnight.
4. Elevate on a microwavable rack and micro-cook on MEDIUM (70%) for 18 minutes or until set. Let stand 10 minutes.

1 Serving				
	Calories	401	Carbohydrate	23 g
	Protein	23 g	Cholesterol	254 mg
	Fat	24 g	Sodium	909 mg

Vegetable Frittata

23 cm (9 inch) pie

This is a delightful main dish to give your leftover vegetables a changed appearance.

500 mL	chopped cooked vegetables	2 cups
175 mL	chopped ham	3/4 cup
10 mL	butter	2 tsp.
1	medium onion, sliced	1
3	green onions, sliced	3
1 clove	garlic, minced	1 clove
125 mL	grated Swiss cheese	1/2 cup
2 mL	salt	1/2 tsp.
4	eggs	4
50 mL	yogurt or milk	1/4 cup

1. Place vegetables in a 23 cm (9 inch) microwavable pie plate. Sprinkle ham evenly over top.
2. Put butter, onions and garlic in a 750 mL (3 cup) microwavable container. Micro-cook on HIGH (100%) for 2 minutes, stirring once. Spread over ham layer and then spread cheese over onions. Sprinkle with salt.
3. Beat eggs with yogurt and pour over top of frittata. Cover loosely with wax paper or parchment paper. Micro-cook on MEDIUM (70%) for 8 minutes or until set.

Note: Green vegetables such as broccoli or spinach are especially nice in this frittata. Make it ahead of time and keep in the refrigerator for several hours before cooking if desired. Increase cooking time to 10 minutes.

1 Serving — 1/6 of pie	Calories	168	Carbohydrate	7 g
	Protein	11 g	Cholesterol	219 mg
	Fat	11 g	Sodium	606 mg

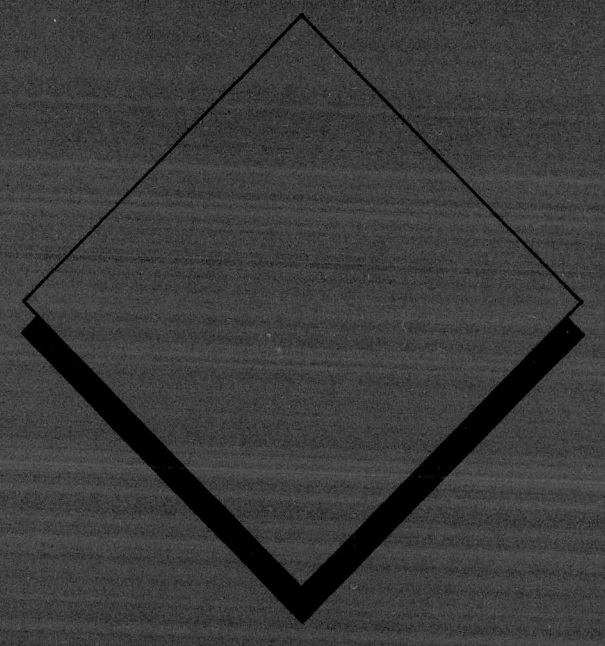

MISCELLANEOUS

Breads
Dressings
Preserves
Sauces
Cereal

Harvard Beets

Serves 4

1 can(540 mL)	canned beets, drained	1 can(19 oz.)
50 mL	sugar	1/4 cup
15 mL	cornstarch	1 Tbsp.
2 mL	salt	1/2 tsp.
2	whole cloves	2
50 mL	cider vinegar	1/4 cup
30 mL	butter	2 Tbsp.

1. Drain beets, reserving 25 mL (2 Tbsp.) juice.
2. Combine reserved juice with sugar, cornstarch, salt, cloves and vinegar in a 750 mL (3 cup) microwavable container. Micro-cook on HIGH (100%) for 2 to 3 minutes, stirring after every minute until thickened.
3. Add beets and butter and stir well. Micro-cook on HIGH (100%) for 1 to 2 minutes or until heated.

1 serving					
	Calories	210	Carbohydrate	40 g
	Protein	1 g	Cholesterol	16 mg
	Fat	6 g	Sodium	571 mg

Chinese Broccoli

Serves 4

1/2 bunch	fresh broccoli, cut into florets	1/2 bunch
50 mL	sliced water chestnuts	1/4 cup
15 mL	soy sauce	1 Tbsp.
15 mL	butter	1 Tbsp.

1. In a small microwavable dish combine soy sauce and butter and micro-cook on HIGH (100%) for 45-60 seconds.
2. Rinse broccoli and arrange in a ring on a round microwavable serving dish. Arrange water chestnuts over top. Cover with plastic wrap and cook about 13 minutes per kg (6 minutes per pound).
3. Remove wrap from broccoli and pour soy mixture over.

1 serving					
	Calories	48	Carbohydrate	4 g
	Protein	2 g	Cholesterol	8 mg
	Fat	3 g	Sodium	298 mg

Broccoli With Sesame Seed Butter

Serves 4

50 mL	butter	1/4 cup
30 mL	sesame seeds	2 Tbsp.
1 bunch	fresh broccoli, cut into florets	1 bunch

1. In a small microwavable dish combine butter and sesame seeds and micro-cook on HIGH (100%) for 2 to 3 minutes or until seeds are lightly browned.
2. Rinse broccoli and arrange in a ring on a round microwavable serving dish. Cover with plastic wrap and cook about 13 minutes per kg (6 minutes per pound) of vegetable.
3. Remove wrap from broccoli and pour seed mixture over.

1 serving	Calories	159	Carbohydrate	6 g
	Protein	4 g	Cholesterol	33 mg
	Fat	15 g	Sodium	149 mg

Broccoli With Hollandaise Sauce

Serves 4

| 1 bunch | fresh broccoli | 1 bunch |
| 1 recipe | Hollandaise sauce (page 190) | 1 recipe |

1. Rinse broccoli and cut into spears. Place on a shallow microwavable serving dish, arranging spears in a ring. Cover with plastic wrap or lid and micro-cook on HIGH (100%) for 13 minutes per kg (6 minutes per pound).
2. Prepare Hollandaise Sauce and pour over.

Note: Another time serve with Cheese Sauce (page 190)

1 serving	Calories	279	Carbohydrate	6 g
	Protein	5 g	Cholesterol	202 mg
	Fat	28 g	Sodium	392 mg

Broccoli Corn Bake

Serves 4

1 pkg.(284 mL)	frozen chopped broccoli	1 pkg.(10 oz.)
25 mL	butter	2 Tbsp.
25 mL	flour	2 Tbsp.
125 mL	milk	$1/2$ cup
1 can(341 mL)	corn niblets	1 can(12 oz.)
1	egg	1
1 mL	celery salt	$1/4$ tsp.

1. Micro-cook broccoli in the package on HIGH (100%) for 6 minutes. Drain.
2. In a 1 L (1 qt.) microwavable casserole melt butter on HIGH. Stir in flour. Add milk and liquid from corn. Micro-cook on HIGH (100%) for 3 minutes or until boiling, stirring once.
3. Beat egg and add a small amount of sauce to egg, then transfer egg mixture back to casserole, blending well. Add celery salt.
4. Combine broccoli and corn with sauce in casserole. Micro-cook on MEDIUM (70%) for 5 minutes or until heated through.

Note: This can be made ahead and kept in the refrigerator until serving time. Heat for 10 minutes on HIGH (100%) if refrigerated.

1 serving				
	Calories	197	Carbohydrate	25 g
	Protein	8 g	Cholesterol	94 mg
	Fat	9 g	Sodium	238 mg

Brussels Sprouts With Herb Cheese Sauce

Serves 4

500 g	Brussels sprouts, trimmed	1 lb.
50 mL	water	¼ cup

1. Combine sprouts and water. Cover and micro-cook on HIGH (100%) for 6 to 8 minutes. Drain. Let stand while preparing sauce.

Herb Cheese Sauce:

15 mL	butter	1 Tbsp.
15 mL	flour	1 Tbsp.
1 mL	dried chervil	¼ tsp.
1 mL	dried basil	¼ tsp.
dash	salt	dash
125 mL	milk	½ cup
50 mL	shredded Swiss Cheese	¼ cup

1. In a small microwavable container melt butter on HIGH. Stir in flour, chervil, basil and salt. Blend in milk. Micro-cook on HIGH (100%) for 2 to 3 minutes or until sauce thickens and boils, stirring several times. Stir in cheese until it is melted. Pour over Brussels sprouts.

1 serving	Calories	100	Carbohydrate	9 g
	Protein	4 g	Cholesterol	16 mg
	Fat	6 g	Sodium	161 mg

Brussels Sprouts With Water Chestnuts

Serves 4

500 g	Brussels sprouts	1 lb.
50 mL	water	¼ cup
50 mL	water chestnuts, sliced	¼ cup
25 mL	chopped parsley	2 Tbsp.
50 mL	butter	3 Tbsp.

1. Trim sprouts. Place in a 1 L (1 qt.) microwavable container and add water. Cover and micro-cook on HIGH (100%) for 6-8 minutes or until tender.
2. Add water chestnuts, parsley and butter. Stir to mix. Cover and let stand 5 minutes.

1 serving	Calories	111	Carbohydrate	7 g
	Protein	2 g	Cholesterol	25 mg
	Fat	9 g	Sodium	112 mg

Maple Glazed Carrot Coins

Serves 4

500 g	thinly sliced carrots	1 lb.
50 mL	water	1/4 cup
50 mL	maple syrup	1/4 cup
25 mL	butter	2 Tbsp.

1. Soak carrots in cold water for 5 to 15 minutes. Drain.
2. In a 1 L (1 qt.) microwavable casserole combine carrots and water. Cover and micro-cook on HIGH (100%) for 8 minutes or until tender. Drain.
3. Stir in maple syrup and butter, blending well. Micro-cook on HIGH (100%), uncovered, for 1 to 2 minutes or until heated through and syrup is slightly thickened.

1 serving	Calories	133	Carbohydrate	20 g
	Protein	1 g	Cholesterol	16 mg
	Fat	6 g	Sodium	92 mg

Glazed Carrot Sticks

Serves 4

500 g	carrot sticks	1 lb.
50 mL	water	1/4 cup
30 mL	butter	2 Tbsp.
5 mL	brown sugar	1 tsp.
1 mL	salt	1/4 tsp.
	parsley for garnish	

1. Cover carrots with cold water and let stand 5 to 15 minutes. Drain.
2. In a 1 L (1 qt.) microwavable casserole combine carrots and water. Cover and micro-cook on HIGH (100%) for 8 minutes. Drain.
3. Stir in remaining ingredients. Garnish with parsley.

1 serving	Calories	79	Carbohydrate	6 g
	Protein	1 g	Cholesterol	16 mg
	Fat	6 g	Sodium	198 mg

Variation: Rosemary Carrots
Add 1 mL (1/4 tsp.) rosemary and 25 mL (2 Tbsp.) chopped chives with butter and brown sugar.

Carottes à l'orange

Serves 4

500 g	**carrots, peeled and**	**1 lb.**
	sliced 3 mm (¹/₈ inch) thick	
50 mL	**water**	**¹/₄ cup**
50 mL	**orange marmalade**	**¹/₄ cup**
5 mL	**lemon juice**	**1 tsp.**
5 mL	**butter**	**1 tsp.**
	chopped parsley	

1. Soak carrots in cold water 5 to 15 minutes. Drain.
2. In a 1 L (1 qt.) microwavable casserole combine carrots and water. Cover and micro-cook on HIGH (100%) for 8 minutes or until tender.
3. Add remaining ingredients and micro-cook on HIGH (100%) for 1 minute longer.

1 serving	Calories	91	Carbohydrate	21 g
	Protein	1 g	Cholesterol	3 mg
	Fat	1 g	Sodium	35 mg

Carrots and Snow Peas

Serves 4

375 mL	**sliced carrots**	**1 ¹/₂ cups**
25 mL	**water**	**2 Tbsp.**
125 g	**snow peas**	**4 oz.**
10 mL	**butter**	**2 tsp.**
10 mL	**sunflower or sesame seeds**	**2 tsp.**
	seasoned salt	

1. Cover carrots with cold water and let stand 5 to 15 minutes. Drain.
2. Combine carrots and water in a 1 L (4 cup) microwavable casserole. Cover and micro-cook on HIGH (100%) for 4 minutes. Add snow peas. Cover and micro-cook on HIGH (100%) 1 ¹/₂ minutes longer or until vegetables are just tender. Drain.
3. Add butter, seeds and a few shakes of seasoned salt. Mix well and let stand 2 to 3 minutes.

1 Serving	Calories	58	Carbohydrate	5 g
	Protein	2 g	Cholesterol	7 mg
	Fat	3 g	Sodium	171 mg

Carrot Celery Medley

Serves 4

500 mL	thinly sliced carrots	2 cups
15 mL	butter	1 Tbsp.
2 mL	lemon juice	$1/2$ tsp.
5 mL	brown sugar	1 tsp.
250 mL	diced celery	1 cup
1 large	onion, chopped	1 large

1. Cover carrots with cold water and let stand 5 to 15 minutes. Drain.
2. Place butter in a 1.5 L (6 cup) microwavable casserole or ring mould. Micro-cook on HIGH (100%) until melted. Add lemon juice and sugar and mix well. Add carrots, celery and onion and mix well. Cover and micro-cook on HIGH (100%) for 6 to 8 minutes or until vegetables are barely tender, stirring after 4 minutes of cooking.

1 serving				
	Calories	69	Carbohydrate	10 g
	Protein	1 g	Cholesterol	8 mg
	Fat	3 g	Sodium	62 mg

Gratinée of Cauliflower

Serves 4

50 mL	butter	$\frac{1}{4}$ cup
50 mL	finely chopped onion	$\frac{1}{4}$ cup
1 head	cauliflower, broken into florets	1 head
30 mL	flour	2 Tbsp.
1 mL	salt	$\frac{1}{4}$ tsp.
175 mL	milk	$\frac{3}{4}$ cup
250 mL	grated Swiss cheese	1 cup
50 mL	chopped fresh parsley	$\frac{1}{4}$ cup

1. In a 3 L (3 qt.) microwavable container micro-cook butter on HIGH (100%) until melted. Add onion and micro-cook on HIGH (100%) about 1 minute or until soft.
2. Slice cauliflower into 6 mm ($\frac{1}{4}$ inch) slices. Add cauliflower to butter mixture. Cover and micro-cook on HIGH (100%) about 6 to 8 minutes or until tender crisp. Remove cauliflower to a 2 L (2 qt.) microwavable casserole, reserving liquid.
3. Add flour and salt to the reserved liquid. Stir in milk and micro-cook on HIGH (100%) until thickened and boiling, about 2 to 3 minutes, stirring frequently. Pour over cauliflower.
4. Just before serving micro-cook on HIGH (100%) until hot and bubbly. Top with cheese. Cover and allow to stand 1 minute to melt cheese. Sprinkle with parsley.

1 serving	Calories	278	Carbohydrate	13 g
	Protein	11 g	Cholesterol	58 mg
	Fat	21 g	Sodium	398 mg

Green Beans With Prosciutto

Serves 4

500 mL	French-style frozen green beans	2 cups
10 mL	oil	2 tsp.
10 mL	chopped shallots or green onions	2 tsp.
50 mL	chopped prosciutto or ham	1/4 cup
	salt and pepper	

1. Place beans in a 1 L (1 qt.) microwavable casserole and micro-cook on HIGH (100%) for 6 minutes or until almost tender. Drain.
2. In a small microwavable container place oil, shallots and prosciutto. Micro-cook on HIGH (100%) for 1 to 2 minutes or until shallots are tender. Stir ham into beans; cover and micro-cook on HIGH (100%) for 2 minutes or until heated through. Check for seasoning and add salt and pepper if desired.

1 serving					
	Calories	73	Carbohydrate	5 g
	Protein	4 g	Cholesterol	5 mg
	Fat	5 g	Sodium	173 mg

Herbed Green Beans

Serves 4

500 mL	French-style frozen green beans	2 cups
50 mL	chopped green pepper	1/4 cup
50 mL	chopped onion	1/4 cup
1	garlic clove, minced	1
1	tomato, chopped	1
15 mL	olive oil	1 Tbsp.
2 mL	salt	1/2 tsp.
1 mL	sugar	1/4 tsp.
2 mL	savory	1/2 tsp.
dash	pepper	dash

1. Place beans in a 1 L (1 qt.) microwavable casserole. Cover and micro-cook beans on HIGH (100%) for 6 minutes. Drain.
2. In a 750 mL (3 cup) microwavable container combine remaining ingredients and micro-cook on HIGH (100%) for 1 1/2 minutes.
3. Combine beans with green pepper mixture. Cover and micro-cook on HIGH (100%) for 2 minutes or until heated through.

1 serving					
	Calories	48	Carbohydrate	9 g
	Protein	2 g	Cholesterol	0 mg
	Fat	1 g	Sodium	244 mg

Orange Glazed Parsnips

Serves 4

Amazingly good even to non-parsnip lovers.

500 g	medium-sized parsnips	1 lb.
50 mL	water	1/4 cup
30 mL	butter	2 Tbsp.
10 mL	cornstarch	2 tsp.
50 mL	brown sugar	1/4 cup
2 mL	salt	1/2 tsp.
0.5 mL	pepper	1/8 tsp.
50 mL	orange juice	1/4 cup
	grated rind of 1/2 orange	

1. Wash and peel parsnips. Cut in julienne sticks. Cover with water in a 1 L (1 qt.) microwavable container and let stand 5 to 15 minutes. Drain and add back 50 mL (1/4 cup) water. Cover and micro-cook on HIGH (100%) for 8 minutes or until tender, stirring once. Let stand while making sauce.
2. In a small microwavable container melt butter on HIGH. Add remaining ingredients and blend well. Micro-cook on HIGH (100%) for 2 to 3 minutes or until thickened, stirring twice.
3. Drain parsnips. Pour sauce over and mix well.

1 serving	Calories	215	Carbohydrate	40 g
	Protein	2 g	Cholesterol	16 mg
	Fat	6 g	Sodium	79 mg

Peas and Mushrooms

Serves 4

30 mL	butter	2 Tbsp.
30 mL	chopped onion	2 Tbsp.
125 mL	sliced mushrooms	1/2 cup
375 g	frozen peas	12 oz.
dash	thyme	dash

1. Place butter in a 1.5 L (6 cup) microwavable casserole. Micro-cook on HIGH (100%) for 30 seconds. Stir in onions and mushrooms and micro-cook on HIGH (100%) for 2 to 2 1/2 minutes until soft.
2. Add peas and thyme. Cover and micro-cook on HIGH (100%) for 6 minutes minutes or until peas are well heated, stirring once. Let stand 3 minutes. Add salt to taste.

1 serving	Calories	128	Carbohydrate	13 g
	Fat	6 g	Cholesterol	16 mg
	Carbohydrate	13 g	Sodium	162 mg

Variation: Peas and Shallots
Substitute 50 mL (1/4 cup) chopped shallots for onions and mushrooms.

Salmon Cups with Parsley Sauce
Peas and Mushrooms
Confetti Rice
Pineapple Squares

Spinach Mushroom Bake

Serves 4

A colourful and delicious way to serve spinach.

1 pkg.(280 g)	fresh spinach	1 pkg.(10 oz.)
375 g	fresh mushrooms	12 oz.
30 mL	melted butter	2 Tbsp.
50 mL	finely chopped onion	1/4 cup
1 mL	garlic salt	1/4 tsp.
	pepper	
125 mL	grated cheese (Cheddar or Swiss)	1/2 cup

1. Wash spinach and remove stems. Shake off excess water and put in a 1 L (1 qt.) microwavable container. Cover and micro-cook on HIGH (100%) for 3 1/2 minutes. Drain well, pressing to remove as much liquid as possible. Place spinach in the bottom of a 2 L (2 qt.) microwavable baking dish.
2. Brush and slice mushrooms. Place butter, mushrooms and onions in same container and micro-cook on HIGH (100%) for 3 minutes. Drain.
3. Sprinkle spinach with garlic salt and pepper. Then sprinkle with half the cheese. Arrange mushrooms over top and sprinkle with remaining cheese. Micro-cook on HIGH (100%) until hot, about 1-2 minutes.

1 Serving					
	Calories	150	Carbohydrate	7 g	
	Protein	7 g	Choleterol	31 mg	
	Fat	11 g	Sodium	322 mg	

Garlic Spinach

Serves 4

1 clove	garlic, minced	1 clove
15 mL	oil	1 Tbsp.
1 pkg.(280 g)	fresh spinach, washed	1 pkg.(10 oz.)

1. In a 1 L (1 qt.) microwavable casserole micro-cook garlic and oil on HIGH (100%) for 1 minute.
2. Mix in spinach. Cover and micro-cook on HIGH (100%) for 4 minutes or until spinach is wilted.

1 serving					
	Calories	49	Carbohydrate	2 g	
	Protein	2 g	Cholesterol	0 mg	
	Fat	4 g	Sodium	53 mg	

Glazed Squash

Serves 4

1 kg	Acorn or Pepper squash	2 lb.
15 mL	brown sugar	1 Tbsp.
15 mL	butter	1 Tbsp.
1 mL	cinnamon	¼ tsp.
1 mL	nutmeg	¼ tsp.
	pepper	

1. Cut squash in half lengthwise and remove seeds. Place cut side down on a shallow microwavable dish. Micro-cook on HIGH (100%) for 15 minutes per kg (7 minutes per pound).
2. Combine remaining ingredients. Turn squash cut side up and cut into four pieces. Spread sugar-butter on surface. Micro-cook on HIGH (100%) 1 minute longer.

1 serving				
	Calories	114	Carbohydrate	21 g
	Protein	3 g	Cholesterol	8 mg
	Fat	4 g	Sodium	39 mg

Turnip Souffle

Serves 4

1 medium	turnip	1 medium
25 mL	sugar	2 Tbsp.
2 mL	salt	½ tsp.
2	eggs, separated	2
30 mL	butter	2 Tbsp.
5 mL	grated orange rind	1 tsp.

1. Pierce turnip. Place on a white paper towel on oven tray or in a 3 L (3 qt.) microwavable container and micro-cook on HIGH (100%) about 13 minutes per kg (6 minutes per pound) or until knife inserts easily. Let stand 5 minutes. Cut in quarters and remove skin.
2. Place turnip, sugar, salt, pepper, egg yolks, butter and orange rind in a food processor. Process until smooth.
3. Beat egg whites until stiff and fold into turnip mixture.
4. Pour into a 1 L (1 qt.) microwavable casserole. Cover and micro-cook on MEDIUM (70%) for 2 to 3 minutes.

1 serving				
	Calories	157	Carbohydrate	15 g
	Protein	4 g	Cholesterol	167 mg
	Fat	9 g	Sodium	412 mg

Vegetable Mornay

Serves 4

3-4	carrots, cut in thin slices	3-4
25 mL	hot water	2 Tbsp.
1/2 bunch	fresh broccoli, in florets	1/2 bunch
1/2 head	fresh cauliflower, in florets	1/2 head
250 mL	fresh mushrooms, sliced	1 cup
50 mL	sliced water chestnuts	1/4 cup
25 mL	butter	2 Tbsp.
25 mL	flour	2 Tbsp.
2 mL	salt	1/2 tsp.
dash	pepper	dash
175 mL	milk	3/4 cup
15 mL	Parmesan cheese	1 Tbsp.
125 mL	grated Swiss Cheese	1/2 cup

1. Soak carrots in water for 5 to 15 minutes. Drain.
2. In a 3 L (3 qt.) microwavable container combine carrots and hot water. Cover and micro-cook on HIGH (100%) for 2 minutes. Add broccoli and cauliflower and micro-cook 5 to 7 minutes, or until almost tender. Stir in mushrooms and water chestnuts and micro-cook on HIGH (100%) 1 minute longer. Drain.
3. Place butter in a 1 L (1 qt.) microwavable casserole. Micro-cook on HIGH (100%) until melted. Blend in flour, salt and pepper. Stir in milk and micro-cook on HIGH (100%) until thickened and boiling, stirring several times. Stir in cheeses until blended.
4. Pour sauce over vegetable mixture and micro-cook on HIGH (100%) for 3 to 5 minutes or until sauce is bubbly and vegetables are hot.

1 serving				
	Calories	208	Carbohydrate	19 g
	Protein	9 g	Cholesterol	31 mg
	Fat	12 g	Sodium	578 mg

Zucchini and Tomatoes

Serves 4

30 mL	butter or margarine	2 Tbsp.
10 mL	fresh chopped parsley	2 tsp.
50 mL	chopped onion	1/4 cup
2 mL	garlic salt	1/2 tsp.
1 mL	dried basil	1/4 tsp.
2	zucchini, 18 cm or 7 inch	2
1	tomato, peeled and chopped or 125 mL (1/2 cup) cherry tomatoes, halved	1
125 mL	grated cheese (Mozzarella, Brick or Cheddar)	1/2 cup
25 mL	dry bread crumbs	2 Tbsp.

1. Place butter in a 1 L (1 qt.) microwavable casserole and melt on HIGH (100%), about 30 seconds. Add parsley and onion and micro-cook on HIGH (100%) for 2 minutes or until onions are tender.
2. Mix in garlic salt and basil, then add zucchini and tomatoes. Cover and micro-cook on HIGH (100%) for 4 minutes or until zucchini is just tender.
3. Sprinkle first with cheese and then bread crumbs. Micro-cook on HIGH (100%) for 1 minute longer or just until cheese is slightly melted.

1 serving				
	Calories	147	Carbohydrate	8 g
	Protein	5 g	Cholesterol	31 mg
	Fat	11 g	Sodium	415 mg

Parsley Rice

Serves 4

250 mL	long grain rice	1 cup
550 mL	hot water	2 1/4 cups
5 mL	chicken bouillon granules	1 tsp.
1 mL	salt	1/4 tsp.
25 mL	chopped fresh parsley	2 Tbsp.

1. Combine rice, water, bouillon and salt in a 2 L (2 qt.) microwavable casserole. Cover and micro-cook on HIGH (100%) for 5 to 6 minutes or until boiling. Reduce power to LOW (30%) and micro-cook for 12 minutes. Stir in parsley and let stand 5 minutes.

1 serving	Calories	184	Carbohydrate	40 g
	Protein	4 g	Cholesterol	0 mg
	Fat	0 g	Sodium	358 mg

Variation: Confetti Rice
Add 30 mL (2 Tbsp.) dried vegetable flakes when cooking rice. Omit parsley.

Teriyaki Rice

Serves 4

500 mL	hot water	2 cups
250 mL	long grain rice	1 cup
50 mL	sliced green onions	1/4 cup
7 mL(1 pkt.)	instant beef bouillon	1 1/2 tsp.(1 pkt.)
25 mL	light soy sauce	2 Tbsp.
25 mL	dry sherry	2 Tbsp
1	clove garlic, minced	1

1. Combine all ingredients in a 2 L (2 qt.) microwavable casserole. Cover and micro-cook on HIGH (100%) for 6 to 8 minutes or until boiling. Reduce power to LOW (30%) and micro-cook for 12 minutes or until water is almost absorbed. Let stand for 10 minutes.

1 serving	Calories	195	Carbohydrate	42 g
	Protein	5 g	Cholesterol	0 mg
	Fat	0 g	Sodium	864 mg

◇ *Rice is generally best cooked with no stirring. After the standing time toss gently with serving spoon to mix.*

Wild Rice and Vegetables

Serves 4

75 mL	wild rice	$^1/_3$ cup
675 mL	hot water	2 $^3/_4$ cups
5 mL	salt	1 tsp.
175 mL	long grain rice	$^3/_4$ cup
2 pkts.	chicken bouillon	2 pkts.
25 mL	butter	2 Tbsp.
1	large onion, chopped	1
125 g	fresh mushrooms, sliced	4 oz.
250 mL	grated carrot	1 cup
1 mL	white pepper	$^1/_4$ tsp.
25 mL	minced fresh parsley	2 Tbsp.

1. Wash wild rice. Combine with water and salt in a 2 L (2 qt.) microwavable casserole. Cover and micro-cook on HIGH (100%) for 5 minutes or until boiling, then on LOW (30%) for 20 minutes.
2. Add long grain rice and bouillon and cook on MEDIUM-LOW (50%) for 15 minutes more.
3. In a 750 mL (3 cup) microwavable container melt butter on HIGH. Add onion and saute on HIGH (100%) for 2 minutes. Add mushrooms, carrots and pepper and micro-cook on HIGH (100%) for 2 minutes. Stir and micro-cook on HIGH (100%) for 1 to 2 minutes longer. Stir vegetables and parsley into rice and let stand for 10 minutes

1 serving					
	Calories	314	Carbohydrate	56 g	
	Protein	8 g	Cholesterol	16 mg	
	Fat	7 g	Sodium	1026 mg	

Wild Rice Medley

Serves 4

25 mL	butter	2 Tbsp.
25 mL	chopped onion	2 Tbsp.
25 mL	chopped celery	2 Tbsp.
25 mL	chopped green pepper	2 Tbsp.
125 mL	brown rice	1/2 cup
50 mL	wild rice	1/4 cup
25 mL	snipped fresh parsley	2 Tbsp.
500 mL	hot water	2 cups
1 pkt.	chicken bouillon granules	1 pkt.
1 mL	salt	1/4 tsp.
1	bay leaf	1

1. Melt butter on HIGH (100%) in bottom of a 2 L (2 qt.) microwavable casserole. Add onion, celery and green pepper and micro-cook on HIGH (100%) for 1 minute. Add remaining ingredients and mix well. Cover and micro-cook on HIGH (100%) for 5 minutes, then on LOW (30%) for 40 minutes or until water is almost absorbed. Let stand, covered, for 5 minutes. Remove bay leaf.

1 serving				
	Calories	225	Carbohydrate	37 g
	Protein	5 g	Cholesterol	16 mg
	Fat	7 g	Sodium	424 mg

Souffle Potatoes

Serves 4

4 medium	potatoes(about 550 g or 18 oz.)	4 medium
5 mL	salt	1 tsp.
dash	pepper	dash
25 mL	finely chopped onion	2 Tbsp.
50 mL	milk	1/4 cup
1	egg, separated	1
	grated Parmesan cheese	
	paprika	

1. Wash potatoes and pierce skins. Place in cups of muffin pan or place on floor of oven arranged in a ring and micro-cook on HIGH (100%) 8 to 10 minutes. Let stand, covered, for 5 minutes.
2. Scoop out potatoes with a spoon and reserve shells. Mash potato with seasonings, milk and egg yolk.
3. Beat egg white until stiff and fold into potato mixture.
4. Refill shells, sprinkle with cheese and paprika.
5. Arrange potatoes on a shallow microwavable serving plate and micro-cook on HIGH (100%) about 2 minutes or until heated.

Note: These freeze well. To serve, defrost in microwave and heat on HIGH (100%) to serving temperature.

1 serving	Calories	145	Carbohydrate	26 g
	Protein	6 g	Cholesterol	77 mg
	Fat	2 g	Sodium	534 mg

Potato Puff

Serves 4

4	baking potatoes(about 550g or 18 oz.)	4
30 mL	finely minced onion	2 Tbsp.
125 g	soft or whipped cream cheese	4 oz.
125 mL	milk	1/2 cup
1	egg white, beaten	1
	grated Parmesan cheese	

1. Place potatoes in cups of muffin pan or arrange in a ring on floor of oven and micro-cook on HIGH (100%) for 8 to 10 minutes. Let stand, covered, for 5 minutes.
2. Peel potatoes, mash, and combine with onion, cheese and milk. Gently stir in beaten egg white. Pour into a 1 L (1 qt.) microwavable casserole. Sprinkle with Parmesan cheese and micro-cook on HIGH (100%) for 2 to 3 minutes or until heated through.

1 serving	Calories	213	Carbohydrate	23 g
	Protein	7 g	Cholesterol	34 mg
	Fat	11 g	Sodium	138 mg

Browned Potato Wedges

Serves 4

4	medium potatoes, peeled and cut in wedges (about 450 g or 1 lb.)	4
50 mL	butter	3 Tbsp.

1. Melt butter in a 1 L (1 qt.) microwavable container on HIGH. Combine with potato wedges. Cover and micro-cook on HIGH (100%) for 5 minutes.
2. Preheat broiler on Combination ovens with broil or a conventional oven. When hot place potatoes in oven pan and broil for 10 minutes or until browned.

1 serving	Calories	170	Carbohydrate	20 g
	Protein	2 g	Cholesterol	25 mg
	Fat	9 g	Sodium	98 mg

Golden Potato Balls

Serves 4

15 mL	flour	1 Tbsp.
5 mL	salt	1 tsp.
5 mL	paprika	1 tsp.
650 g	large potatoes (4 to 5)	24 oz.
50 mL	butter	1/4 cup
	chopped parsley	

1. Combine flour, salt and paprika. Set aside.
2. Peel potatoes.
3. Preheat a large browning dish on HIGH (100%) for 6 minutes.
4. Using a melon baller, cut out evenly shaped balls from the potatoes. Roll between paper towels to dry. Coat with flour mixture.
5. When dish is hot add butter and quickly toss in potatoes to coat. Micro-cook on HIGH (100%) for 5 minutes or until potatoes are tender. Sprinkle with parsley.

1 serving	Calories	205	Carbohydrate	22 g
	Protein	3 g	Cholesterol	33 mg
	Fat	12 g	Sodium	606 mg

Cheese Potatoes

Serves 4

450 g	peeled potatoes	1 lb.
125 mL	butter	1/2 cup
125 mL	Parmesan cheese	1/2 cup
5 mL	garlic salt	1 tsp.
2 mL	paprika	1/2 tsp.
50 mL	flour	1/4 cup

1. Cut each potato evenly into 6 or 8 wedges depending on size.
2. Melt butter and dip potatoes to coat with butter. Place in a shallow microwavable baking dish.
3. Combine cheese, salt, paprika and flour. Sprinkle evenly over potatoes. Mix gently.
4. Cover with parchment or wax paper and micro-cook on HIGH (100%) for 8 to 10 minutes or until tender. Stir several times.

1 serving	Calories	380	Carbohydrate	27 g
	Protein	8 g	Cholesterol	73 mg
	Fat	27 g	Sodium	907 mg

Parsley Potatoes

Serves 4

4	peeled medium potatoes (about 450 g or 1 lb.)	4
50 mL	butter	1/4 cup
25 mL	chopped fresh parsley	2 Tbsp.

1. Cut potatoes into wedges.
2. Melt butter in a shallow microwavable baking dish on HIGH. Stir in potatoes to coat with butter. Cover with parchment or wax paper. Micro-cook on HIGH (100%) for 8 to 10 minutes or until potatoes are soft, stirring frequently. Sprinkle with parsley.

1 serving	Calories	197 g	Carbohydrate	20 g
	Protein	3 g	Cholesterol	33 mg
	Fat	12 g	Sodium	129 mg

Potato and Pepper Ratatouille

Serves 4

500 g	peeled potatoes (5 medium)	16 oz.
250 g	zucchini (1 large)	8 oz.
1	red or green pepper, cored and seeded	1
1	onion	1
1 mL	pepper	1/4 tsp.
25 mL	oil	2 Tbsp.
25 mL	dark soy sauce	2 Tbsp.
25 mL	water	2 Tbsp.

1. Slice potatoes paper thin (1 mm), slice other vegetables 2 mm (1/8 inch) thick.
2. Combine remaining ingredients in the bottom of a 1.5 L (1.5 qt.) microwavable casserole. Mix in vegetables.
3. Cover and micro-cook on HIGH (100%) about 12 minutes or until vegetables are tender-crisp. Serve hot.

Note: If potatoes are sliced thicker than 1 mm, precook on HIGH (100%) for 1-2 minutes.

1 serving	Calories	267	Carbohydrate	45 g
	Protein	6 g	Cholesterol	0 mg
	Fat	8 g	Sodium	522 mg

Horseradish Potatoes and Cream

Serves 4

30 mL	prepared horseradish	2 Tbsp.
15 mL	instant chicken bouillon granules	1 Tbsp.
5 mL	all-purpose flour	1 tsp.
1 mL	salt	1/4 tsp.
dash	pepper	dash
250 mL	half and half or cereal cream	1 cup
750 mL	peeled potatoes, cut in 1 cm (1/4 inch) cubes	3 cups
	fresh parsley (optional)	

1. In a 1.5 L (6 cup) microwavable ring mould combine horseradish, bouillon, flour, salt and pepper. Mix well.
2. Blend in cream.
3. Stir in potatoes. Cover and micro-cook on MEDIUM (70%) for 20 minutes or until potatoes are tender, stirring twice.
4. Let stand for 5 minutes. Garnish with parsley if desired.

1 serving	Calories	178	Carbohydrate	24 g
	Protein	5 g	Cholesterol	23 mg
	Fat	7 g	Sodium	630 mg

Potatoes and Sour Cream

Serves 4

4	medium potatoes	4
	about 550 g or 18 oz.	
2	eggs, well beaten	2
250 mL	sour cream	1 cup
30 mL	milk	2 Tbsp.
50 mL	chopped green onions or chives	1/4 cup
2 mL	salt	1/2 tsp.
dash	freshly ground pepper	dash

1. Place potatoes in cups of muffin pan or place on floor of oven arranged in a ring. Micro-cook potatoes on HIGH (100%) for 12 minutes or until almost cooked. Let stand 5 minutes.
2. Peel potatoes and slice.
3. Combine eggs with sour cream, milk, onions, salt and pepper.
4. Place half of potato slices in a 1 L (1 qt.) microwavable casserole. Pour half of cream mixture over. Repeat with remaining potatoes and cream. Micro-cook on MEDIUM (70%) for 3 minutes, then on LOW (30%) for 4 minutes or until almost set. Let stand 5 minutes.

1 serving				
	Calories	270	Carbohydrate	28 g
	Protein	8 g	Cholesterol	188 mg
	Fat	14 g	Sodium	313 mg

Scalloped Potatoes

Serves 4

45 mL	butter	3 Tbsp.
45 mL	finely chopped onion	3 Tbsp.
45 mL	flour	3 Tbsp.
2 mL	salt	1/2 tsp.
dash	pepper	dash
375 mL	milk	1 1/2 cups
750 mL	thinly sliced potatoes	3 cups
	bread crumbs	
	chopped parsley	

1. In a 750 mL (3 cup) microwavable container melt butter on HIGH. Stir in onions, flour and seasonings.
2. Micro-cook milk on HIGH (100%) for 2 1/2 to 3 minutes. Blend into flour mixture and micro-cook on HIGH (100%) until mixture just comes to a boil, stirring every 30 seconds.
3. Place half of potatoes in bottom of 1.5 L (6 cup) microwavable ring mould. Cover with half of sauce. Repeat layers. Cover and micro-cook on HIGH (100%) for 4 minutes, then on LOW (30%) for 7 minutes or until potatoes are soft. Let stand 5 minutes.
4. Sprinkle with bread crumbs and chopped parsley before serving.

Note: For a thicker consistency, remove cover during last minute of cooking.

1 serving	Calories	268	Carbohydrate	36 g
	Protein	7 g	Cholesterol	32 mg
	Fat	11 g	Sodium	383 mg

Green Fettuccine Alfredo

Serves 4

375 g	green fettuccine	12 oz.
75 mL	cream	1/3 cup
50 mL	grated Parmesan cheese	1/4 cup

1. Bring 1.5 L (6 cups) hot salted water to a boil in a 3 L (3 qt.) microwavable container.
2. Add fettuccine and micro-cook on HIGH (100%) for 6-10 minutes or until fettuccine is tender but firm. Drain and rinse with hot water.
3. Mix in cream and cheese. Serve immediately.

1 Serving	Calories	372	Carbohydrate	64 g
	Protein	13 g	Cholesterol	17 mg
	Fat	6 g	Sodium	106 mg

SWEET ENDINGS

Desserts
Cakes
Squares
Candy

Orange Cream Dessert

Serves 4

7 mL	unflavoured gelatin	1 $^1/_2$ tsp.
50 mL	sugar	$^1/_4$ cup
50 mL	milk	$^1/_4$ cup
1	egg yolk	1
30 mL	fresh lemon juice (1 lemon)	2 Tbsp.
45 mL	orange juice	3 Tbsp.
15 mL	orange liqueur	1 Tbsp.
50 mL	sieved cottage cheese	$^1/_4$ cup
50 mL	flaked coconut	$^1/_4$ cup
1	egg white	1
125 mL	whipping cream	$^1/_2$ cup
1 can	mandarin oranges	1 can

1. Mix gelatin and sugar in a 750 mL (3 cup) microwavable container. Blend in milk and egg yolk. Micro-cook on HIGH (100%) about 40 seconds or until gelatin is dissolved and mixture begins to thicken. Stir twice.
2. Add lemon juice, orange juice, liqueur, cottage cheese and coconut. Chill until partially set — about 45 minutes. Stir.
3. Beat egg whites until stiff. Whip cream until stiff. Fold egg white and cream into chilled mixture. Spoon into a glass serving dish or individual parfait glasses, alternating cream with oranges. Reserve a few oranges for garnishing the top.

1 Serving				
	Calories	221	Carbohydrate	25 g
	Protein	6 g	Cholesterol	91 mg
	Fat	11 g	Sodium	92 mg

Lemon Cream Layers

Serves 8

50 mL	butter or margarine	1/4 cup
300 mL	graham or gingersnap crumbs	1 1/4 cup
15 mL	sugar	1 Tbsp.
250 mL	sugar	1 cup
75 mL	cornstarch	1/3 cup
250 mL	water	1 cup
	grated rind of 1 lemon	
75 mL	fresh lemon juice (2 lemons)	1/3 cup
15 mL	butter or margarine	1 Tbsp.
2	egg yolks	2
250 mL	whipping cream, whipped	1 cup
125 mL	icing sugar	1/2 cup
125 g	cream cheese	4 oz.
2	egg whites	2

1. Place first amount of butter in an 20x20 cm (8x8inch) microwavable dish. Micro-cook on HIGH (100%) until melted. Stir in crumbs and first amount of sugar. Press onto bottom and micro-cook on HIGH (100%) for 1 1/2 minutes or until slightly browned and set.
2. In a 750 mL (3 cup) microwavable container combine second amount of sugar and cornstarch. Blend in water. Micro-cook on HIGH (100%) until thick and clear, about 4 to 5 minutes, stirring several times. Blend in lemon rind, juice and second amount of butter. Stir until well blended. Blend in yolks. Micro-cook on HIGH (100%) 1 minute or until thickened. Place in freezer for 5 to 10 minutes or until cooled but not set.
3. Meanwhile beat cream until stiff. Soften cheese on LOW (30%) and beat with icing sugar. Gently fold into whipped cream. Spread over crumb mixture.
4. Beat egg whites until stiff and fold in lemon mixture. Spread over cheese mixture. Chill until serving time.

1 Serving					
	Calories	407	Carbohydrate	54 g	
	Protein	4 g	Cholesterol	132 mg	
	Fat	21 g	Sodium	213 mg	

◆ *Micro-cook lemon on HIGH for 20 seconds before squeezing to extract the maximum amount of juice.*

Veal Cordon Bleu
Wild Rice with Vegetables
Orange Cream Dessert

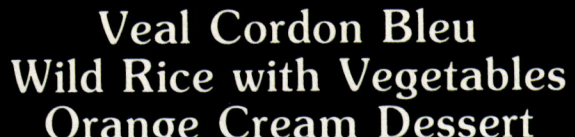

Floating Islands

Serves 4

425 mL	milk	1 ²/₃ cups
30 mL	cornstarch	2 Tbsp.
dash	salt	dash
50 mL	sugar	¹/₄ cup
2	egg yolks	2
5 mL	vanilla	1 tsp.
2	egg whites	2
50 mL	sugar	¹/₄ cup

1. In a 500 mL (2 cup) microwavable container, micro-cook milk on HIGH (100%) for 3 minutes or until hot but not boiling.
2. Combine cornstarch, salt and first amount of sugar in a 1 L (1 qt.) microwavable container. Blend in milk slowly, stirring well. Micro-cook on MEDIUM (70%) for 2 minutes or until boiling, stirring after 1 ¹/₂ minutes.
3. Beat egg yolks to blend and stir a small amount of hot mixture into yolks. Blend well and return yolk mixture to hot mixture, mixing well. Micro-cook on MEDIUM (70%) 1 minute longer or until thickened. Stir in vanilla. Pour into 4 individual microwavable serving dishes.
4. Beat egg whites until foamy. Gradually add second amount of sugar, beating until stiff peaks form.
5. Drop in 4 mounds over each pudding. Micro-cook on MEDIUM (70%) for 1 to 1 ¹/₂ minutes or until set.

Note: For other flavour variations: Stir 15 mL (1 Tbsp.) orange or other liqueur in place of vanilla, or add 1 square semi-sweet chocolate to pudding in step 3.

1 Serving				
	Calories	229	Carbohydrate	39 g
	Protein	7 g	Cholesterol	158 mg
	Fat	5 g	Sodium	89 mg

Pineapple Cheesecake

23 cm (9 inch) pie

50 mL	butter or margarine	1/4 cup
300 mL	graham or vanilla wafer crumbs	1 1/4 cup
30 mL	sugar	2 Tbsp.
375 g	cream cheese	12 oz.
25 mL	milk	2 Tbsp.
50 mL	sugar	1/4 cup
15 mL	lemon juice	1 Tbsp.
2	eggs, beaten	2
30 mL	cornstarch	2 Tbsp.
50 mL	sugar	1/4 cup
1 can(398 mL)	crushed pineapple	1 can(14 oz.)
15 mL	lemon juice	1 Tbsp.

1. Micro-cook butter in a 23 cm (9 inch) microwavable pie plate or quiche dish on HIGH (100%) until melted. Add crumbs and first amount of sugar and blend with butter. Press firmly onto bottom and up sides of plate. Micro-cook on HIGH (100%) for 1 1/2 minutes to set.
2. Place cream cheese and milk in a 1 L (4 cup) microwavable container and micro-cook on MEDIUM (70%) for 1 minute to soften. Beat in second amount of sugar, lemon juice and eggs. Pour into pie shell. Elevate on a microwavable rack and micro-cook on MEDIUM (70%) for 8 minutes or until set. Chill until firm.
3. Make topping: In a 750 mL (3 cup) glass measure combine cornstarch and third amount of sugar. Stir in pineapple and juice. Micro-cook on HIGH (100%) until mixture begins to thicken and comes to a boil, about 4 minutes. Stir just before mixture comes to a boil and once after. Stir in lemon juice. Cool and spread over cheesecake.

Note: This may also be made in individual custard cups or ramekins. Reduce cooking time in step 2 depending on size of cups.

1 Serving	Calories	378	Carbohydrate	39 g
	Protein	6 g	Cholesterol	138 mg
	Fat	23 g	Sodium	275 mg

Chocolate Hazelnut Mini-Cheesecakes

Serves 12

Crust:

100 mL	chocolate cookie crumbs	6 Tbsp.
30 mL	melted butter or margarine	2 Tbsp.
50 mL	ground hazelnuts	3 Tbsp.

1. Place large muffin papers in a vented microwavable muffin pan.
2. Mix crust ingredients together and press $1/12$ of the mixture into each paper. Repeat, making 12 crusts. Set aside.

Filling:

4 squares	semi-sweet chocolate	4 oz.
250 g	cream cheese	8 oz.
75 mL	sugar	$1/3$ cup
1	egg	1
2 mL	vanilla	$1/2$ tsp.
10 mL	Frangelico liqueur (hazelnut)	2 tsp.
75 mL	sour cream	$1/3$ cup
dash	salt	dash

1. Place cream cheese in small microwavable container with chocolate on top. Micro-cook on MEDIUM-LOW (50%) for 3 to 5 minutes until chocolate is just softened. Do not overheat.
2. Combine chocolate with remaining filling ingredients and mix well. Pour over prepared crusts. Micro-cook, 6 at a time, on MEDIUM (70%) for 4 minutes or until set. Chill until firm.

Glaze:

2 squares	semi-sweet chocolate	2 oz.
30 mL	whipping cream	2 Tbsp.
7 mL	Frangelico liqueur	1 $1/2$ tsp.
12	whole hazelnuts for garnish	12

1. Melt chocolate in a small microwavable container on MEDIUM-LOW (50%) for 3 to 4 minutes, stirring once. Add cream and liqueur and stir well.
2. Spread glaze on chilled cheesecakes (remove muffin papers first if desired) and top each cheesecake with a hazelnut. Chill until serving time. These are best if made 1 to 3 days ahead and may be frozen.

Note: The Frangelico liqueur (hazelnut) is available in tiny 50 mL bottles, more than enough for this recipe.

1 Serving	Calories	224	Carbohydrate	17 g
	Protein	3 g	Cholesterol	57 mg
	Fat	17 g	Sodium	90 mg

Frozen Chocolate Tortoni Torte

Serves 12

250 mL	half and half or cereal cream	1 cup
3	egg yolks	3
125 mL	sugar	1/2 cup
dash	salt	dash
5 squares	semi-sweet chocolate	5 oz.
125 mL	Amaretto liqueur	1/2 cup
3	egg whites	3
0.5 mL	cream of tartar	1/8 tsp.
50 mL	sugar	1/4 cup
375 mL	whipping cream	1 1/2 cups
250 mL	amaretti or other macaroon cookie crumbs	1 cup
125 mL	whipping cream	1/2 cup
15 mL	cocoa	1 Tbsp.
25 mL	icing sugar	2 Tbsp.

1. Micro-cook cream on HIGH (100%) for 2 minutes.
2. Meanwhile in a 1 L (1 qt.) microwavable container combine egg yolks, sugar and salt. Gradually whisk in cream. Micro-cook on MEDIUM-LOW (50%) for 2 1/2 minutes or until slightly thickened and mixture coats a metal spoon. Stir every 15 seconds during last minute of cooking. Cut up chocolate and stir in, blending until melted. Stir in liqueur. Cool to room temperature.
3. Beat egg whites with cream of tartar until frothy. Gradually add 50 mL (1/4 cup) sugar 5 mL (1 tsp.) at a time, beating until mixture holds stiff peaks. Fold into chocolate mixture.
4. Whip cream and fold into chocolate mixture along with cookie crumbs.
5. Pour into a lightly oiled 25 cm (10 inch) springform pan and freeze until firm.
6. Blend 125 mL (1/2 cup) cream with cocoa and icing sugar and beat until stiff.
7. Remove cake from pan by running a thin knife around inside edge of pan and lifting out cake. Pipe chocolate cream around edge of cake and garnish with chocolate coffee bean candies or chocolate leaves if desired.

1 Serving	Calories	361	Carbohydrate	41 g
	Protein	4 g	Cholesterol	118 mg
	Fat	20 g	Sodium	107 mg

Kahlua Pie

23 cm (9 inch) pie

Crust:

50 mL	**butter or margarine**	**¼ cup**
300 mL	**graham crumbs**	**1 ¼ cup**
30 mL	**sugar**	**2 Tbsp.**

1. Melt butter in a deep 23 cm (9 in.) microwavable pie plate on HIGH. Combine with crumbs and sugar. Press onto bottom and sides of pie plate. Micro-cook on HIGH (100%) for 1 ½ minutes or until slightly browned and set.

Filling:

250 g	**marshmallows**	**10 oz.**
125 mL	**milk**	**½ cup**
5 mL	**instant coffee powder**	**1 tsp.**
50 mL	**Kahlua liqueur**	**¼ cup**
250 mL	**whipping cream, whipped**	**1 cup**

1. Combine marshmallows and milk in a 3 L (3 qt.) microwavable container. Micro-cook on HIGH (100%) for 2 to 3 minutes until melted, stirring frequently. Stir in coffee powder. Chill until slightly thickened.
2. Fold in Kahlua and whipped cream. Pour into prepared pie shell and chill.

1 Serving				
	Calories	347	Carbohydrate	54 g
	Protein	2 g	Cholesterol	38 mg
	Fat	13 g	Sodium	170 mg

Florida Key Lime Pie

23 cm (9 inch) pie

This is the famous Florida dessert adapted for microwave. If Key Limes are not available ordinary limes will make a delicious dessert.

50 mL	butter or margarine	1/4 cup
300 mL	graham crumbs	1 1/4 cups
30 mL	sugar	2 Tbsp.
1 pkt.	unflavoured gelatin	1 pkt.
175 mL	fresh lime juice (5-6 limes)	3/4 cup
5	egg yolks	5
1 can(300 mL)	sweetened condensed milk	1 can(10 oz.)
5 mL	grated lime rind	1 tsp.
3	egg whites	3
1 mL	cream of tartar	1/4 tsp.
125 mL	sugar	1/2 cup

1. In a 23 cm (9 inch) microwavable pie plate melt butter on HIGH (100%). Stir in crumbs and sugar. Mix well and press on bottom and sides of pie plate. Micro-cook on HIGH (100%) for 1 1/2 minutes.
2. Soften gelatin in lime juice in a 750 mL (3 cup) microwavable container. Set aside.
3. Beat yolks until they are very thick and ribbon from beaters.
4. Micro-cook lime juice on HIGH (100%) for 1 1/2 minutes. Quickly pour in a steady stream into beaten yolks, beating constantly. Mix in milk and rind. Pour into crumb crust.
5. Beat whites with cream of tartar until frothy; gradually beat in sugar until mixture will form stiff peaks. Carefully spoon over filling. Micro-cook on MEDIUM (70%) for 2 minutes. Chill until serving time.

1 Serving					
	Calories	371	Carbohydrate	54 g	
	Protein	8 g	Cholesterol	202 mg	
	Fat	15 g	Sodium	228 mg	

Easy Fruit Flan

Serves 6

1 can (284g)	canned pears	1 can (10 oz.)
25 mL	butter	2 Tbsp.
25 mL	pear juice	2 Tbsp.
50 mL	sugar	1/4 cup
	grated rind of 1 lemon	
250 mL	all-purpose flour	1 cup
100 mL	brown sugar	1/3 cup + 2 Tbsp.
5 mL	baking powder	1 tsp.
1 mL	salt	1/4 tsp.
1 mL	cinnamon	1/4 tsp.
1 mL	nutmeg	1/4 tsp.
1	egg	1
15 mL	oil	1 Tbsp.
125 mL	milk	1/2 cup
1	kiwi fruit	1
	sweetened whipped cream	

1. Line bottom of a 20 cm (8 inch) round microwavable baking dish with parchment or wax paper.
2. Drain pears, reserving juice, and slice thinly.
3. Combine butter, pear juice and sugar in a 750 mL (3 cup) microwavable container and micro-cook at HIGH (100%) for 2 minutes or until sugar is dissolved.
4. Pour mixture into prepared dish and arrange sliced pears on top. Sprinkle with lemon rind.
5. Combine flour, sugar, baking powder, salt, cinnamon and nutmeg. Combine egg, oil, and milk and blend with flour mixture. Pour over fruit. Cover with parchment or wax paper and micro-cook on MEDIUM (70%) for 6 1/2 minutes or until cake tests done.
6. Allow to stand 5 minutes. Invert onto serving dish. Garnish with kiwi slices and sweetened whipped cream.

1 Serving					
	Calories	298	Carbohydrate	55 g
	Protein	4 g	Cholesterol	64 mg
	Fat	7 g	Sodium	155 mg

Fresh Fruit Meringues

Serves 4-6

250 mL	red grapes, seedless or with seeds removed	1 cup
250 mL	green grapes, seedless or with seeds removed	1 cup
250 mL	sliced canned peaches	1 cup
250 mL	sliced canned pears	1 cup
2	oranges, peeled and sliced	2
15 mL	orange liqueur	1 Tbsp.
250 mL	peach and pear juice	1 cup
2	egg whites	2
50 mL	sugar	1/4 cup

1. Combine fruits, liqueur and juice in a flat serving dish.
2. Beat egg whites. Add sugar gradually. Beat until stiff. Drop onto brown paper or parchment. Using a cutting board as support, slide paper into bottom of microwave. Micro-cook on MEDIUM (70%) for 1 to 2 minutes or until set. Slide paper back onto a board and remove from oven. Lift onto top of fruit. Chill until serving time.

1 Serving				
	Calories	181	Carbohydrate	46 g
	Protein	2 g	Cholesterol	0 mg
	Fat	0 g	Sodium	23 mg

Apple Amber

Serves 6

1 L	apples, pared and sliced	4 cups
125 mL	sugar	1/2 cup
50 mL	soft butter	1/4 cup
	grated rind and juice of 1 lemon	
3	eggs, separated	3
5 mL	water	1 tsp.
1 mL	cream of tartar	1/4 tsp.
90 mL	sugar	1/3 cup + 1 Tbsp.

1. In a 23 cm (9inch) quiche dish place apples, sugar, butter, lemon juice and rind. Cover and micro-cook on HIGH (100%) for 4 to 6 minutes or until apples are fork tender. Crush apples with a fork.
2. Beat egg yolks and water. Add to hot apples and micro-cook on MEDIUM (70%) for 3 minutes. Stir once or twice.
3. Preheat Combination oven or regular oven to 400°F.
4. Beat egg whites with cream of tartar. Add sugar very gradually and continue beating until meringue is stiff and glossy. Cover fruit with meringue.
5. Place dish on oven rack and bake at 400°F for 9 to 10 minutes on convection mode or 20 minutes in a regular oven until golden. Serve warm.

Note: To cook meringues in microwave: In step 5 micro-cook on MEDIUM (70%) for 1-2 minutes or until meringue is set. Sprinkle with toasted coconut, if desired, to give colour.

1 Serving				
	Calories	321	Carbohydrate	54 g
	Protein	4 g	Cholesterol	172 mg
	Fat	12 g	Sodium	122 mg

Apple Crisp

Serves 4-6

1.5 L	sliced apples	6 cups
125 mL	all-purpose flour	1/2 cup
75 mL	oatmeal	1/3 cup
75 mL	brown sugar	1/3 cup
50 mL	butter or margarine	1/4 cup
3 mL	cinnamon	1/2 tsp.

1. Place apples in a deep 20 cm (8inch) round or square microwavable baking dish.
2. Combine remaining ingredients until crumbly and sprinkle over top of apples.
3. Micro-cook on HIGH (100%) for 8-10 minutes or until apples are tender.

Note: For easy single servings make double or triple quantities of topping mixture and store in refrigerator. For each serving slice one apple into a 175 mL (6 oz.) custard cup and sprinkle with a generous 50 mL (1/4 cup) of topping. Micro-cook on HIGH (100%) about 2 minutes or until tender.

1 Serving					
	Calories	270	Carbohydrate	48 g
	Protein	2 g	Cholesterol	22 mg
	Fat	9 g	Sodium	87 mg

Dark brown sugar gives more colour than does regular brown sugar for microwave cooking.

Rhubarb Crunch

Serves 6-8

1 L	diced rhubarb	4 cups
175 mL	sugar	³/₄ cup
30 mL	cornstarch	2 Tbsp.
175 mL	water	³/₄ cup
5 mL	vanilla	1 tsp.
175 mL	all-purpose flour	³/₄ cup
175 mL	oatmeal	³/₄ cup
175 mL	brown sugar	³/₄ cup
125 mL	butter or margarine	¹/₂ cup
5 mL	cinnamon	1 tsp.

1. Place rhubarb in a 20 cm (8 inch) round or square microwavable baking dish.
2. Combine sugar and cornstarch in a 750 mL (3 cup) microwavable container. Blend in water. Micro-cook on HIGH (100%) until boiling, about 2-3 minutes, stirring several times. Stir in vanilla and pour over rhubarb.
3. Combine remaining ingredients and blend until crumbly. Spread over rhubarb. Micro-cook on HIGH (100%) for 15 minutes or until bubbly.

1 Serving				
	Calories	362	Carbohydrate	60 g
	Protein	3 g	Cholesterol	33 mg
	Fat	13 g	Sodium	130 mg

Caribbean Bananas

Serves 4

25 mL	butter	2 Tbsp.
2	large bananas	2
25 mL	brown sugar	2 Tbsp.
2 mL	cinnamon	1/2 tsp.
25 mL	orange flavoured liqueur	2 Tbsp.
50 mL	orange juice	1/4 cup
25 mL	dark rum	2 Tbsp.

1. Place butter in a 2 L (2 qt.) microwavable baking dish. Micro-cook on HIGH (100%) until butter melts. Slice bananas lengthwise and roll in butter.
2. Mix brown sugar and cinnamon. Sprinkle over bananas.
Micro-cook on HIGH (100%) for 2 minutes or until sugar begins to melt.
3. Add liqueur and juice. Micro-cook on HIGH (100%) for 30 seconds. Let stand.
4. Heat rum in a small microwavable cup on HIGH (100%) for 10 to 15 seconds. BE SURE NOT TO LET BOIL. Pour over bananas and quickly touch lighted match to rum to ignite. Serve over ice cream.

1 Serving				
	Calories	216	Carbohydrate	36 g
	Protein	1 g	Cholesterol	16 mg
	Fat	7 g	Sodium	65 mg

Cherries Jubilee

Serves 4

1 can(540 mL)	dark sweet cherries	1 can(19 oz.)
25 mL	cornstarch	1 1/2 Tbsp.
75 mL	sugar	1/3 cup
5 mL	lemon juice	1 tsp.
500 mL	vanilla ice cream	2 cups

1. Drain cherries. Combine juice with cornstarch and sugar in a 750 mL (3 cup) microwavable container. Micro-cook on HIGH (100%) for 2 1/2 to 3 minutes. Stir in lemon juice and then cherries. Serve over ice cream.

1 Serving				
	Calories	252	Carbohydrate	58 g
	Protein	2 g	Cholesterol	10 mg
	Fat	3 g	Sodium	25 mg

◆ *To flambe a dessert, micro-cook 25 mL (2 Tbsp.) liqueur on HIGH for 15 seconds. Be sure liquid does not boil. Pour over dessert and light with a match.*

Almond Float

Serves 4

A simple, light dessert that goes nicely with Chinese foods.

50 mL	sugar	1/4 cup
1 envelope	unflavoured gelatin	1 envelope
425 mL	milk	1 3/4 cup
5 mL	almond extract	1 tsp.
1 can	mandarin oranges	1 can

1. In a 750 mL (3 cup) microwavable container combine sugar and gelatin. Add half of milk and micro-cook on HIGH (100%) until gelatin dissolves, about 2 minutes. Stir in remaining milk and almond extract.
2. Pour into a 20x20 cm (8x8 inch) square dish and chill.

Sauce:

250 mL	hot water	1 cup
50 mL	sugar	1/4 cup
2 mL	almond extract	1/2 tsp.

1. Combine water and sugar in a 750 mL (3 cup) microwavable container and micro-cook on HIGH (100%) until sugar is dissolved, about 1 minute. Stir in extract. Chill.

To serve: Cut gelatin in squares and place in a glass serving bowl. Pour sauce over. Drain oranges and add to bowl. Garnish with fresh mint if available.

1 Serving				
	Calories	124	Carbohydrate	25 g
	Protein	4 g	Cholesterol	5 mg
	Fat	1 g	Sodium	38 mg

Zabaglione

Serves 4

An easy, elegant dessert

4	egg yolks	4
100 mL	sugar	$1/2$ cup
50 mL	sherry or Marsala	$1/4$ cup
4	egg whites	4

1. Combine egg yolks and sugar in a 750 mL (3 cup) microwavable container and beat until creamy. Micro-cook on MEDIUM (70%) about 60 seconds or until slightly thickened.
2. Stir in sherry or Marsala. Micro-cook on MEDIUM (70%) about 20 seconds or until thickened.
3. Beat egg whites and fold into yolk mixture. Serve immediately in tall, stemmed glasses.

1 Serving	Calories	243	Carbohydrate	33 g
	Protein	7 g	Cholesterol	301 mg
	Fat	6 g	Sodium	76 mg

Butterscotch Pudding

Serves 4

500 mL	milk	2 cups
125 mL	brown sugar	$1/2$ cup
30 mL	cornstarch	2 Tbsp.
1 mL	salt	$1/4$ tsp.
1	egg, slightly beaten	1
30 mL	butter or margarine	2 Tbsp.
2 mL	vanilla extract	$1/2$ tsp.

1. In a 500 mL (2 cup) microwavable container, micro-cook milk on HIGH (100%) for 4 $1/2$ minutes or until hot but not boiling.
2. In a 1 L (1 qt.) microwavable container, blend together brown sugar, cornstarch and salt. Gradually blend in milk, mixing well. Micro-cook on HIGH (100%) for 1 to 2 minutes, stirring every 30 seconds until mixture is smooth and thickened and has come to a boil.
3. Stir a small amount of the hot pudding quickly into the beaten egg, then add to the pudding, mixing well. Micro-cook on MEDIUM (70%) for 1 minute, stirring after 30 seconds, until smooth and thickened.
4. Stir in butter and vanilla. Pour into serving dishes. Chill.

1 Serving	Calories	250	Carbohydrate	35 g
	Protein	6 g	Cholesterol	101 mg
	Fat	10 g	Sodium	267 mg

Baked Rice Pudding

Serves 6

This is delicious served slightly warm with pure maple syrup.

375 mL	milk	1 1/2 cups
2	eggs	2
75 mL	sugar	1/3 cup
dash	salt	dash
5 mL	vanilla	1 tsp.
500 mL	cooked rice	2 cups
75 mL	raisins	1/3 cup

1. In a 500 mL (2 cup) microwavable container, micro-cook milk on HIGH (100%) for 3 minutes or until hot but not boiling.
2. Meanwhile beat eggs well and stir in sugar, salt and vanilla. Gradually stir in milk. Blend in rice and raisins.
3. Pour into a lightly oiled 1.5 L (6 cup) microwavable ring mould. Cover and micro-cook on LOW (30%) for 14 minutes or until set. Let stand until almost cold.

1 Serving	Calories	177	Carbohydrate	31 g
	Protein	6 g	Cholesterol	105 mg
	Fat	3 g	Sodium	241 mg

◇When cooked rice is required, 250 mL (1 cup) uncooked rice will yield approximately 875 mL (3 1/2 cups) cooked rice.

Rum and Raisin Bread Pudding

Serves 6

1 L	brown bread cubes (about 6 slices)	4 cups
125 mL	raisins	1/2 cup
dash	salt	dash
2 mL	nutmeg	1/2 tsp.
375 mL	milk	1 1/2 cups
3	eggs	3
125 mL	brown sugar	1/2 cup
50 mL	rum	3 Tbsp.
	Custard Sauce (page 191) or sweetened whipped cream	

1. Place bread in a lightly oiled 2 L (2 qt.) round microwavable baking dish. Sprinkle raisins, salt and nutmeg over top.
2. In a 500 mL (2 cup) microwavable container, micro-cook milk on HIGH (100%) for 3 minutes.
3. Meanwhile blend eggs, sugar and rum. Stir in milk and pour over bread cubes. Cover with parchment or wax paper.
4. Micro-cook on MEDIUM (70%) for 7 minutes or until set.
5. Serve either warm or cold with Custard Sauce or sweetened whipped cream.

1 Serving				
	Calories	202	Carbohydrate	39 g
	Protein	6 g	Cholesterol	151 mg
	Fat	4 g	Sodium	124 mg

◇ *To soften hard brown sugar, place a piece of bread and the sugar in a microwavable container. Cover and micro-cook on HIGH for 30 seconds to 1 minute or until sugar is softened.*

Maple Trifle

Serves 12

1 recipe	Sponge Cake	1 recipe
1 recipe	Custard	1 recipe
1 can(540 mL)	pear halves	1 can(19 oz.)
125 mL	maple syrup	1/2 cup
250 mL	whipping cream	1 cup
30 mL	maple syrup	2 Tbsp.

1. Cut cake into 1.5 cm (1/2 inch) slices and place half of slices in a large glass serving bowl.
2. Drain pears reserving 125 mL (1/2 cup) juice. Combine juice with first amount of maple syrup and pour half over cake layer.
3. Slice pears and layer half over cake. Top with half of custard. Repeat layers and chill.
4. Just before serving whip cream until stiff. Fold in second amount of syrup and spoon or pipe over top of cake.

Sponge Cake:

125 mL	sugar	1/2 cup
125 mL	butter or margarine	1/2 cup
2	eggs	2
30 mL	water	2 Tbsp.
2 mL	maple flavour	1/2 tsp.
250 mL	all-purpose flour	1 cup
5 mL	baking powder	1 tsp.
1 mL	salt	1/4 tsp.

1. Cream sugar and butter together. Add eggs, water and maple flavour.
2. Mix flour, baking powder and salt. Pour into a 1.5 L (6 cup) microwavable ring mould. Cover with parchment or wax paper and micro-cook on MEDIUM (70%) for 4 minutes or until almost dry on top. Let stand in pan 5 minutes and turn out.

Custard:

375 mL	milk	1 1/2 cups
3	eggs	3
50 mL	brown sugar	3 Tbsp.
15 mL	maple syrup	1 Tbsp.

1. In a 500 mL (2 cup) microwavable container, micro-cook milk on HIGH (100%) for 3 minutes or until hot but not boiling.
2. Beat eggs, sugar and syrup in a 750 mL (3 cup) microwavable container. Whisk hot milk into egg mixture, blending well. Micro-cook on HIGH (100%) for 1 1/2 to 2 minutes, stirring after each 30 seconds, until thickened. Do not allow to boil or it will curdle. Cool.

1 Serving	Calories	342	Carbohydrate	47 g
	Protein	5 g	Cholesterol	163 mg
	Fat	15 g	Sodium	189 mg

Gâteau Allemande Framboise
(Raspberry Sponge Cake)

Serves 6

6	eggs, separated	6
275 mL	sugar	1 cup + 2 Tbsp.
	grated rind of 1 lemon	
75 mL	fresh lemon juice	1/3 cup
125 mL	all-purpose flour	1/2 cup
75 mL	cream of wheat	1/3 cup
50 mL	ground almonds	1/4 cup
2 mL	almond extract	1/2 tsp.
25 mL	sherry	2 Tbsp.
375 mL	raspberries	1 1/2 cups
375 mL	whipping cream, whipped and sweetened	1 1/2 cups
175 mL	slivered almonds, toasted	3/4 cup

1. Line bottoms of two 2 L (2 qt.) round thermoplastic cake pans with parchment or wax paper.
2. Beat egg yolks and sugar until very thick and creamy. Blend in lemon rind, lemon juice (reserving 5 mL [1 tsp.]), flour, cream of wheat, almonds and almond extract.
3. Beat egg whites with reserved lemon juice until they form stiff peaks. Fold whites gently but thoroughly into egg yolk mixture.
4. Spoon equal amounts of batter into each dish and spread evenly. Cover with parchment or wax paper and micro-cook cakes one at a time on MEDIUM (70%) for 4 to 5 minutes or just until dry on surface. Rotate if necessary. Allow to stand 10 minutes.
5. Invert cakes onto a cooling rack and remove paper. Allow to cool.
6. Place one layer on a serving dish and sprinkle with sherry. Top with half the raspberries and about 1/3 of the sweetened whipped cream. Place second layer on top. Cover with remaining berries and cream. Sprinkle with almonds.

Note: To toast almonds, place on a microwavable dish and micro-cook on HIGH (100%) for 3 to 5 minutes or until slightly browned, stirring frequently.

1 Serving				
	Calories	542	Carbohydrate	76 g
	Protein	12 g	Cholesterol	342 mg
	Fat	23 g	Sodium	93 mg

Brazilian Banana Cake

Serves 6-8

75 g	Brazil nuts	3 oz.
75 mL	shortening	1/3 cup
125 mL	sugar	1/2 cup
1	egg	1
125 mL	mashed banana	1/2 cup
5 mL	lemon juice	1 tsp.
75 mL	milk	1/3 cup
2 mL	vanilla	1/2 tsp.
250 mL	all-purpose flour	1 cup
2 mL	baking powder	1/2 tsp.
2 mL	baking soda	1/2 tsp.
1 mL	salt	1/4 tsp.
250 mL	whipping cream, whipped and sweetened	1 cup

1. Line bottom of a 2 L (2 qt.) round thermoplastic cake pan with parchment or wax paper.
2. Cover nuts with hot water and drain. Slice 3 mm (1/8 inch) thick. Place on a baking dish and toast on HIGH (100%) about 5 to 6 minutes or until slightly browned. Stir several times.
3. Cream shortening and sugar. Beat in egg and banana. Add lemon juice, milk, and vanilla. Combine flour with baking powder, soda and salt and stir in. Pour into prepared pan. Cover with parchment or wax paper and micro-cook on MEDIUM (70%) for 6 to 7 minutes or until cake tests done. Allow to stand 10 minutes. Unmould onto serving plate.
4. Slice cake into two layers. Spread whipped cream on bottom half. Place top layer on top and spread with remaining cream. Sprinkle with toasted nuts.

1 Serving				
	Calories	375	Carbohydrate	38 g
	Protein	6 g	Cholesterol	59 mg
	Fat	23 g	Sodium	200 mg

◇ *Doneness test for cakes: There are two main criteria for judging doneness of cakes 1) the cake is just starting to pull away from the side of the pan 2) there is only a slight amount of moisture remaining on the surface of the cake.*

Date Cake With Penuche Frosting

Serves 6-8

250 mL	boiling water	1 cup
250 mL	finely chopped dates	1 cup
125 mL	butter or margarine	1/2 cup
250 mL	sugar	1 cup
1	egg	1
300 mL	all-purpose flour	1 1/4 cups
1 mL	salt	1/4 tsp.
5 mL	baking powder	1 tsp.
5 mL	baking soda	1 tsp.
250 mL	chopped nuts	1 cup

1. Pour boiling water over dates. Let stand.
2. Line bottom of a 2 L (2 qt.) round thermoplastic cake pan with parchment or wax paper.
3. Cream butter and sugar, add egg.
4. Combine flour, salt, baking powder and soda. Blend into creamed mixture, then add nuts and date mixture. Stir until well blended.
5. Pour into prepared pan and cover with parchment or wax paper. Micro-cook on MEDIUM (70%) for 9 to 10 minutes or until cake tests done. Let stand 5 minutes and turn out onto serving platter.

Penuche Frosting:

50 mL	butter	1/4 cup
125 mL	brown sugar	1/2 cup
30 mL	milk	2 Tbsp.
375 mL	icing sugar	1 1/2 cups

1. Combine butter and brown sugar in a 750 mL (3 cup) microwavable container. Micro-cook on HIGH (100%) for 1 minute.
2. Stir in milk and micro-cook on HIGH (100%) 2 minutes longer. Blend in icing sugar and spread over warm cake.

1 Serving				
	Calories	638	Carbohyrate	109 g
	Protein	5 g	Cholesterol	87 mg
	Fat	23 g	Sodium	498 mg

Oatmeal Spice Cake With Coconut Pecan Topping

Serves 6

300 mL	boiling water	1 1/4 cups
250 mL	oatmeal	1 cup
125 mL	butter	1/2 cup
250 mL	white sugar	1 cup
175 mL	brown sugar	3/4 cup
2	eggs	2
5 mL	vanilla	1 tsp.
375 mL	all-purpose flour	1 1/2 cups
5 mL	baking soda	1 tsp.
5 mL	cinnamon	1 tsp.
5 mL	nutmeg	1 tsp.

1. Pour boiling water over oatmeal. Let stand 10 minutes.
2. Line bottom of a 2 L (2 qt.) round thermoplastic cake pan with parchment or wax paper.
3. Cream butter and sugars. Add eggs and vanilla and mix well.
4. Mix dry ingredients and add to creamed mixture alternately with oats.
5. Pour into prepared pan. Cover with parchment or wax paper and micro-cook on MEDIUM (70%) for 10 to 11 minutes or until cake tests done. Let stand 5 minutes and turn out.

Topping:

175 mL	brown sugar	3/4 cup
50 mL	butter	1/4 cup
30 mL	milk	2 Tbsp.
125 mL	coconut	1/2 cup
125 mL	chopped pecans	1/2 cup

1. Combine sugar, butter and milk in a 750 mL (3 cup) microwavable container. Micro-cook on HIGH (100%) for 1 1/2 to 2 minutes or until boiling. Micro-cook on HIGH (100%) 1 minute longer. Stir in nuts and coconut and spread over cake.

1 Serving	Calories	767	Carbohydrate	111 g
	Protein	7 g	Cholesterol	166 mg
	Fat	35 g	Sodium	606 mg

Chocolate Upside Down Cake

Serves 6

50 mL	butter or margarine	1/4 cup
125 mL	brown sugar	1/2 cup
125 mL	flaked coconut	1/2 cup
125 mL	granola	1/2 cup
50 mL	butter or margarine	1/4 cup
250 mL	brown sugar	1 cup
1	egg	1
2 mL	vanilla	1/2 tsp.
250 mL	all-purpose flour	1 cup
75 mL	cocoa	1/3 cup
1 mL	salt	1/4 tsp.
3 mL	baking soda	3/4 tsp.
175 mL	milk	3/4 cup

1. Line bottom of a 2 L (2 qt.) round thermoplastic cake pan with parchment or wax paper. Place first amount of butter in dish and micro-cook on HIGH (100%) for 30 seconds or just until melted. Mix brown sugar, coconut and granola and spread evenly to cover bottom of dish.
2. Cream second amount of butter and sugar in a mixing bowl. Add egg and vanilla.
3. Combine dry ingredients and add to creamed mixture alternately with milk. Pour batter over topping.
4. Cover with wax paper and micro-cook on MEDIUM (70%) for 10 to 11 minutes or until cake tests done. Let stand 5 minutes and turn out.

1 Serving				
	Calories	561	Carbohydrate	79 g
	Protein	7 g	Cholesterol	96 mg
	Fat	27 g	Sodium	526 mg

Apple Ginger Upside Down Cake

Serves 6

50 mL	butter	3 Tbsp.
75 mL	brown sugar	1/3 cup
1	large apple	1
300 mL	all-purpose flour	1 1/4 cups
4 mL	baking powder	3/4 tsp.
2 mL	baking soda	1/2 tsp.
5 mL	ginger	1 tsp.
1 mL	salt	1/4 tsp.
75 mL	butter or margarine	1/3 cup
75 mL	sugar	1/3 cup
1	egg	1
75 mL	milk	1/3 cup
50 mL	molasses	1/4 cup

1. In a 1.5 L (6 cup) thermoplastic ring mould melt first amount of butter. Sprinkle brown sugar over. Peel apple and cut into 16 slices. Arrange over brown sugar.
2. Combine flour, baking powder, soda, ginger and salt.
3. Cream butter and sugar. Add egg, milk and molasses. Stir in dry ingredients. Pour into prepared pan. Cover with parchment or wax paper and micro-cook on MEDIUM (70%) for 6 to 7 minutes or until cake tests done. Let stand 5 minutes and turn out onto serving plate.

1 Serving	Calories	430	Carbohydrate	61 g
	Protein	5 g	Cholesterol	99 mg
	Fat	19 g	Sodium	445 mg

T — A round pan is best for any baking done in your microwave. If you use a ring mould cooking is even faster since it allows microwaves to penetrate from both inside and outside.

Fruit Upside Down Cake

Serves 6

Use either blueberry or pineapple for a delicious fruit topped cake.

Cake:

1	egg	1
175 mL	brown sugar	3/4 cup
75 mL	soft shortening	1/3 cup
300 mL	all-purpose flour	1 1/4 cups
10 mL	baking powder	2 tsp.
2 mL	salt	1/2 tsp.
2 mL	cinnamon	1/2 tsp.
50 mL	milk	1/4 cup
50 mL	orange or pineapple juice	1/4 cup
5 mL	vanilla	1 tsp.

1. Make either blueberry or pineapple topping in bottom of a 1.5 L (6 cup) thermoplastic ring mould.
2. Beat egg, sugar and shortening.
3. Add dry ingredients, then milk, juice and vanilla. Mix until blended. Spoon carefully over fruit in bottom of pan. Cover with parchment or wax paper and micro-cook on MEDIUM (70%) for 6 to 7 minutes or until cake tests done. Let stand 5 minutes and turn out on a flat plate.

Blueberry Topping:

250 mL	frozen blueberries	1 cup
30 mL	sugar	2 Tbsp.
15 mL	lemon juice	1 Tbsp.

1. In a 1.5 L (6 cup) ring mould combine berries, sugar and lemon juice. Micro-cook on HIGH (100%) for 2 minutes or until berries are thawed.

Pineapple Topping:

50 mL	butter	1/4 cup
75 mL	brown sugar	1/3 cup
1 can(398mL)	pineapple slices	1 can(14 oz.)

1. Place butter in a 1.5 L (6 cup) thermoplastic ring mould. Micro-cook on HIGH (100%) until melted, about 30 seconds. Stir in brown sugar.
2. Drain pineapple, reserving juice for use in cake. Cut each slice in half and arrange halves over top of brown sugar mixture.

1 Serving Cake with Blueberry Topping					
	Calories	390	Carbohydrate	58 g	
	Protein	5 g	Cholesterol	51 mg	
	Fat	16 g	Sodium	194 mg	

1 Serving Cake with Pineapple Topping					
	Calories	523	Carbohydrate	74 g	
	Protein	5 g	Cholesterol	73 mg	
	Fat	24 g	Sodium	278 mg	

Gingerbread With Orange Cream Cheese Topping

Serves 6

75 mL	soft shortening	1/3 cup
30 mL	sugar	2 Tbsp.
1	egg	1
175 mL	molasses	3/4 cup
125 mL	hot water	1/2 cup
325 mL	all-purpose flour	1 1/3 cups
5 mL	baking soda	1 tsp.
2 mL	salt	1/2 tsp.
5 mL	ginger	1 tsp.
5 mL	cinnamon	1 tsp.

1. Mix shortening, sugar and egg. Blend in molasses and then water.
2. Combine dry ingredients and stir in.
3. Pour into 1.5 L (6 cup) thermoplastic ring mould. Cover with parchment or wax paper and micro-cook on MEDIUM for 5 1/2 to 6 1/2 minutes or until cake tests done. Let stand 5 minutes and turn out.

Orange Cream Cheese Topping:

125 g	cream cheese	4 oz.
250 mL	icing sugar	1 cup
30 mL	orange juice	2 Tbsp.

1. Blend cheese and sugar. Stir in orange juice.
2. Serve over warm gingerbread.

1 Serving	Calories	511	Carbohydrate	74 g
	Protein	6 g	Cholesterol	71 mg
	Fat	22 g	Sodium	563 mg

Zucchini Chocolate Cake

Serves 6

50 mL	chocolate chips	1/4 cup
50 mL	butter or margarine	1/4 cup
175 mL	brown sugar	3/4 cup
1	egg	1
2 mL	vanilla	1/2 tsp.
75 mL	milk	1/3 cup
5 mL	lemon juice	1 tsp.
300 mL	all-purpose flour	1 1/4 cups
5 mL	baking soda	1 tsp.
1 mL	salt	1/4 tsp.
30 mL	cocoa	2 Tbsp.
250 mL	grated zucchini	1 cup

1. Sprinkle chips evenly over the bottom of a 1.5 L (6 cup) thermo-plastic ring mould.
2. Cream butter, sugar, egg and vanilla. Combine milk and lemon juice and stir in.
3. Combine flour, soda, salt and cocoa and stir in. Blend in zucchini and pour into prepared pan.
4. Cover with parchment or wax paper and micro-cook on MEDIUM (70%) for 7 to 8 minutes or until cake tests done. Let stand 10 minutes. Unmould onto serving plate.

1 Serving				
	Calories	331	Carbohydrate	53 g
	Protein	6 g	Cholesterol	73 mg
	Fat	12 g	Sodium	514 mg

Chocolate Cupcakes

12 cupcakes

These are tasty cupcakes that do not rise in peaks during cooking. Top with your favourite icing.

50 mL	cocoa	1/4 cup
125 mL	hot water	1/2 cup
50 mL	oil	1/4 cup
1	egg	1
200 mL	all-purpose flour	3/4 cup + 2 Tbsp.
175 mL	sugar	3/4 cup
2 mL	baking soda	1/2 tsp.
1 mL	salt	1/4 tsp.

1. Mix cocoa and water until smooth. Add oil and egg.
2. Mix dry ingredients and stir into cocoa mixture. Mix well.
3. Place paper liners in a microwavable muffin pan and fill half full. Micro-cook on HIGH (100%) for 2 1/2 minutes or until just dry on top.

1 Serving				
	Calories	152	Carbohydrate	24 g
	Protein	2 g	Cholesterol	25 mg
	Fat	6 g	Sodium	125 mg

Pecan Bourbon Cake

18 servings

Pecans and bourbon combine to give a cake with a delightful and unusual flavour — elegant enough for the most discriminating guest.

8	pecan halves	8
325 mL	finely chopped pecans	1 1/3 cups
250 mL	butter	1 cup
375 mL	sugar	1 1/2 cups
4	eggs	4
5 mL	lemon extract	1 tsp.
50 mL	bourbon	1/4 cup
425 mL	all-purpose flour	1 2/3 cups
2 mL	salt	1/2 tsp.
2 mL	baking powder	1/2 tsp.
3 mL	baking soda	3/4 tsp.

1. Place pecan halves in bottom of 3 L (12 cup) thermoplastic tube pan.
2. Cream butter and sugar until well blended. Beat in eggs one at a time, mixing well after each. Mix in lemon extract and bourbon.
3. Combine flour, salt, baking powder and soda. Add to butter mixture along with remaining nuts. Spoon into prepared pan.
4. Cover with parchment or wax paper and place on a microwavable rack. Micro-cook on MEDIUM (70%) for 10 1/2 to 11 1/2 minutes or until cake tests done. Let stand for 10 minutes and turn out onto serving platter.

1 Serving	Calories	250	Carbohydrate	31 g
	Protein	3 g	Cholesterol	96 mg
	Fat	13 g	Sodium	258 mg

◇*To cook a large cake (equivalent to two layers) it is essential to use a 3 L (12 cup) ring mould. Otherwise it will not cook in the centre before the edges are overcooked.*

Carrot Cake With Cream Cheese Glaze

Serves 12

375 mL	all-purpose flour	1 1/2 cups
375 mL	sugar	1 1/2 cups
7 mL	baking powder	1 1/2 tsp.
5 mL	baking soda	1 tsp.
10 mL	cinnamon	2 tsp.
1 mL	nutmeg	1/4 tsp.
250 mL	oil	1 cup
4	eggs	4
500 mL	shredded carrots	2 cups
125 mL	raisins	1/2 cup

1. Combine flour, sugar, baking powder, soda, cinnamon and nutmeg.
2. Combine oil and eggs. Stir in flour mixture. Stir in carrots and then raisins. Pour into a 3 L (12 cup) thermoplastic tube pan. Cover and elevate on a microwavable rack and micro-cook on MEDIUM (70%) for 13 to 14 minutes or until cake tests done. Let stand 10 minutes. Unmould and drizzle with glaze when cool.

Cream Cheese Glaze:

60 g	cream cheese	2 oz.
25 mL	milk	2 Tbsp.
5 mL	vanilla	1 tsp.
250 mL	icing sugar	1 cup

1. In a 750 mL (3 cup) microwavable container soften cheese with milk on LOW (30%) for 1 minute.
2. Combine with remaining ingredients.
3. Drizzle over cake while slightly warm.

Note: Half of this recipe cooks nicely in a 1.5 L (6 cup) microwavable ring mould. Micro-cook on MEDIUM (70%) for 8 to 9 minutes. Use the other half for muffins: micro-cook 6 at a time on HIGH (100%) for 2 1/2 minutes in a microwavable muffin pan lined with paper liners.

1 Serving	Calories	499	Carbohydrate	64 g
	Protein	5 g	Cholesterol	106 mg
	Fat	26 g	Sodium	207 mg

Applesauce Cake

Serves 12

500 mL	all-purpose flour	2 cups
300 mL	sugar	1 ¼ cups
7 mL	baking soda	1 ½ tsp.
1 mL	salt	¼ tsp.
5 mL	cinnamon	1 tsp.
2 mL	nutmeg	½ tsp.
1 mL	ground cloves	¼ tsp.
250 mL	shortening	1 cup
250 mL	applesauce	1 cup
4	eggs	4
50 mL	milk	¼ cup
125 mL	raisins	½ cup

1. Mix dry ingredients together in processor or mixer bowl. Add shortening and cut in.
2. Add applesauce, eggs and milk. Mix just until blended (about 10 on/off pulses in food processor). Stir in raisins.
3. Turn batter into a 3 L (12 cup) thermoplastic tube pan and place on a microwavable rack. Cover with parchment or wax paper and micro-cook on MEDIUM (70%) for 13 ½ to 14 ½ minutes or until cake is almost dry on top. Let stand 10 minutes and turn out onto serving plate.
4. When cool drizzle with Lemon Glaze.

Lemon Glaze:

30 mL	butter	2 Tbsp.
15 mL	lemon juice	1 Tbsp.
250 mL	icing sugar	1 cup

1. Combine butter and lemon juice in a small microwavable container. Micro-cook on HIGH (100%) for 30 seconds until butter is melted.
2. Stir in icing sugar and micro-cook on HIGH (100%) for 20 seconds. Beat with a spoon to blend. Drizzle over cooled cake.

For cupcakes: Spoon batter into a microwavable muffin pan lined with paper liners. Micro-cook 6 at a time on HIGH (100%) for 2 ½ to 3 minutes.

1 Serving				
	Calories	481	Carbohydrate	62 g
	Protein	5 g	Cholesterol	106 mg
	Fat	25 g	Sodium	330 mg

Apricot Cake

Serves 12

50 mL	graham cracker crumbs	1/4 cup
250 mL	chopped dried apricots	1 cup
375 mL	orange juice	1 1/2 cups
125 mL	butter or margarine	1/2 cup
425 mL	all-purpose flour	1 3/4 cups
250 mL	firmly packed brown sugar	1 cup
50 mL	whole wheat flour	1/4 cup
7 mL	baking powder	1 1/2 tsp.
5 mL	baking soda	1 tsp.
2 mL	salt	1/2 tsp.
2 mL	nutmeg	1/2 tsp.
2 mL	cinnamon	1/2 tsp.
1 mL	ginger	1/4 tsp.
5 mL	vanilla	1 tsp.
2	eggs	2

1. In a 750 mL (3 cup) microwavable container combine chopped apricots and orange juice. Add butter. Micro-cook on HIGH (100%) for 3 minutes. Let stand.

2. In a food processor or by hand, combine remaining dry ingredients. Pulse 2 to 3 times to blend. Add apricot mixture, eggs and vanilla. Pulse 5 to 6 times to blend.

3. Pour batter into a 3 L (12 cup) thermoplastic tube pan. Cover with parchment or wax paper and elevate on a microwavable rack. Micro-cook on MEDIUM (70%) for 9 to 10 minutes or until cake tests done. Let stand 10 minutes and turn out. Drizzle glaze over.

Glaze:

60 g	cream cheese	2 oz.
25 mL	orange juice	2 Tbsp.
10 mL	grated orange peel	2 tsp.
250 mL	icing sugar	1 cup

1. Soften cheese with orange juice in a small microwavable container on LOW (30%) for 1 minute. Combine with remaining ingredients and blend well.

1 serving	Calories	322	Carbohydrate	52 g
	Protein	5 g	Cholesterol	77 mg
	Fat	11 g	Sodium	368 mg

Apple Mince Squares

16 squares

300 mL	quick-cooking rolled oats	1 1/4 cups
250 mL	all-purpose flour	1 cup
125 mL	brown sugar	1/2 cup
2 mL	nutmeg	1/2 tsp.
125 mL	butter or margarine	1/2 cup
250 mL	mincemeat	1 cup
500 mL	finely chopped, tart baking apples, cored and peeled	2 cups
15 mL	brandy	1 Tbsp.

1. Combine oats, flour, sugar and nutmeg. With pastry blender or food processor cut in butter until mixture is crumbly. Press half of mixture evenly onto bottom of a 2 L (2 qt.) microwavable cake pan. Cover with lid or parchment paper and micro-cook on MEDIUM (70%) for 3 to 4 minutes or until set.
2. Combine mincemeat, apples and brandy. Spoon evenly over crust. Press remaining oat mixture evenly over top.
3. Cover as before and micro-cook on MEDIUM (70%) for 8 minutes or until top begins to crack. Remove cover and micro-cook on HIGH (100%) for 2 minutes. Allow to cool before cutting into squares.

1 Serving				
	Calories	204	Carbohydrate	32 g
	Protein	2 g	Cholesterol	17 mg
	Fat	8 g	Sodium	81 mg

It is always best to use a round pan for baking in your microwave oven. However, if your oven has an even distribution of microwave energy you may also get successful results using a square pan.

Kahlua Bars

24 bars

Base:

2 squares	unsweetened chocolate	2 oz.
125 mL	butter or margarine	$1/2$ cup
125 mL	sugar	$1/2$ cup
125 mL	brown sugar	$1/2$ cup
2	eggs	2
5 mL	vanilla	1 tsp.
175 mL	all-purpose flour	$3/4$ cup
2 mL	baking powder	$1/2$ tsp.

1. Combine chocolate and butter in a 1 L (1 qt.) microwavable container and micro-cook on MEDIUM-LOW (50%) for 3 minutes or until melted. Stir until smooth. Blend in sugars. Beat in eggs one at a time. Stir in vanilla, then flour and baking powder.
2. Spread in a 2L (2 qt.) microwavable baking dish. Cover with parchment or wax paper and micro-cook on HIGH (100%) 5 $1/2$ to 6 $1/2$ minutes or until top is no longer doughy, rotating dish once if needed. Cool completely.

Filling:

5 mL	instant coffee	1 tsp.
30 mL	Kahlua liqueur	2 Tbsp.
125 mL	butter	$1/2$ cup
500 mL	icing sugar	2 cups

1. Dissolve coffee in Kahlua.
2. Micro-cook butter in a small microwavable container on HIGH (100%) 15 to 30 seconds until softened. Add to sugar and beat with mixer at medium speed. Gradually add Kahlua mixture, beating until smooth and creamy. Spread evenly over cooled base. Refrigerate to set filling.

Frosting:

250 mL	semi-sweet chocolate bits	1 cup
30 mL	oil	2 Tbsp.

1. Combine frosting ingredients in a 750 mL (3 cup) microwavable container.
2. Micro-cook on HIGH (100%) 1 $1/2$ to 2 minutes or until glossy. Stir until smooth. Spread evenly over filling. Refrigerate to set. Store in refrigerator. Allow to stand at room temperature 10 minutes before cutting into bars.

1 Serving	Calories	221	Carbohydrate	27 g
	Protein	2 g	Cholesterol	47 mg
	Fat	12 g	Sodium	100 mg

Cream of Mushroom Soup
Tuna Salad Pita Pockets

Cream of Mushroom Soup (p. 48)
Tuna Salad Pita Pockets (p. 92)

Pineapple Squares

16 squares

Crust:

175 mL	butter or margarine	3/4 cup
50 mL	white sugar	1/4 cup
375 mL	all-purpose flour	1 1/2 cups
1 mL	salt	1/4 tsp.

1. Cream together butter and sugar. Add flour and salt and mix until thoroughly blended. Press into a 2 L (2 qt.) microwavable cake pan. Cover with parchment or wax paper and micro-cook on MEDIUM (70%) for 7 to 8 minutes or until surface is dry and crust flaky. Rotate a quarter turn if necessary.

Topping:

1 can(540 mL)	crushed pineapple	1 can(19 oz.)
1	egg	1
175 mL	brown sugar	3/4 cup
2 mL	salt	1/2 tsp.
2 mL	vanilla	1/2 tsp.
125 mL	toasted coconut	1/2 cup

1. Drain pineapple and spread over baked crust.
2. Beat together egg, brown sugar, salt and vanilla. Stir in coconut. Spread evenly over pineapple. Micro-cook on MEDIUM (70%) for 11 to 12 minutes until surface is bubbly. Rotate if necessary. While still warm, mark into squares. Cool before removing from pan.

To toast coconut: Place coconut in a small microwavable dish. Micro-cook on HIGH (100%) until lightly toasted, about 1 to 3 minutes. Stir very frequently.

1 Serving	Calories	229	Carbohydrate	31 g
	Protein	2 g	Cholesterol	43 mg
	Fat	11 g	Sodium	190 mg

Cherry Squares

16 squares

A colourful square for your holiday sweet tray.

375 mL	all-purpose flour	1 $\frac{1}{2}$ cups
50 mL	brown sugar	$\frac{1}{4}$ cup
175 mL	butter or margarine	$\frac{3}{4}$ cup
1	egg	1
125 mL	brown sugar	$\frac{1}{2}$ cup
125 mL	coconut	$\frac{1}{2}$ cup
125 mL	red or green candied cherries, halved	$\frac{1}{2}$ cup

1. Combine flour, 50 mL ($\frac{1}{4}$ cup) brown sugar and butter. Press into a 2 L (2 qt.) microwavable cake pan. Cover with parchment or wax paper and micro-cook on MEDIUM (70%) for 6 to 7 minutes or until set and dry.
2. Beat egg and stir in 125 mL ($\frac{1}{2}$ cup) brown sugar, coconut and cherries. Spread over base. Micro-cook on MEDIUM (70%) for 5 to 5 $\frac{1}{2}$ minutes or until set and browned. Let cool and cut into squares.

1 Serving				
	Calories	203	Carbohydrate	27 g
	Protein	2 g	Cholesterol	39 mg
	Fat	10 g	Sodium	85 mg

Chocolate Chip Squares

16 squares

425 mL	all-purpose flour	1 $\frac{3}{4}$ cups
5 mL	baking powder	1 tsp.
1 mL	salt	$\frac{1}{4}$ tsp.
250 mL	semi-sweet chocolate chips	1 cup
250 mL	brown sugar	1 cup
125 mL	oil	$\frac{1}{2}$ cup
2	large eggs	2
3 mL	vanilla	$\frac{1}{2}$ tsp.
15 mL	milk	1 Tbsp.

1. Combine flour, baking powder and salt. Stir in chips.
2. Combine sugar, oil, eggs, vanilla and milk. Stir in flour mixture.
3. Spread in a 2 L (2 qt.) microwavable cake pan. Cover with lid or parchment or wax paper and micro-cook on MEDIUM (70%) for 7 to 7 $\frac{1}{2}$ minutes or until surface loses its moist appearance. Allow to stand 5 minutes. Cool before cutting.

1 Serving				
	Calories	218	Carbohydrate	29 g
	Protein	3 g	Cholesterol	38 mg
	Fat	10 g	Sodium	61 mg

Peanut Butter Squares

16 squares

50 mL	butter or margarine	1/4 cup
50 mL	smooth peanut butter	1/4 cup
175 mL	brown sugar	3/4 cup
2	eggs	2
250 mL	all-purpose flour	1 cup
2 mL	baking powder	1/2 tsp.
1 mL	salt	1/4 tsp.
5 mL	vanilla	1 tsp.

1. Combine margarine and peanut butter. Stir in sugar, mixing well. Stir in eggs and vanilla.
2. Stir in flour, baking powder and salt.
3. Spread in a 2 L (2 qt.) microwavable cake pan. Cover with lid or parchment or wax paper and micro-cook on MEDIUM (70%) for 4 1/2 to 5 minutes or until surface loses its moist appearance. Cool and cut into squares.

1 Serving					
	Calories	120	Carbohydrate	15 g	
	Protein	3 g	Cholesterol	46 mg	
	Fat	6 g	Sodium	88 mg	

Spice Bars

16 bars

250 mL	all-purpose flour	1 cup
125 mL	sugar	1/2 cup
2 mL	baking soda	1/2 tsp.
2 mL	cinnamon	1/2 tsp.
2 mL	nutmeg	1/2 tsp.
2 mL	allspice	1/2 tsp.
1 mL	cloves	1/4 tsp.
1 mL	salt	1/4 tsp.
125 mL	water	1/2 cup
125 mL	oil	1/2 cup
1	egg	1
125 mL	raisins	1/2 cup
	icing sugar	

1. Combine dry ingredients in a bowl. Combine water, oil and egg and mix with dry ingredients.
2. Spread in a 2 L (2 qt.) microwavable cake pan. Sprinkle raisins over top. Cover with parchment or wax paper and micro-cook on MEDIUM (70%) for 6 1/2 to 7 minutes or until surface loses its moist appearance.
3. Cool and sprinkle with icing sugar. Cut into bars.

1 Serving					
	Calories	157	Carbohydrate	21 g	
	Protein	2 g	Cholesterol	19 mg	
	Fat	8 g	Sodium	95 mg	

Brownies

16 squares

125 mL	butter or margarine	$1/2$ cup
2	eggs	2
250 mL	sugar	1 cup
5 mL	vanilla	1 tsp.
175 mL	all-purpose flour	$3/4$ cup
1 mL	baking powder	$1/4$ tsp.
1 mL	salt	$1/4$ tsp.
125 mL	cocoa	$1/2$ cup

1. Place butter in a 1 L (1 qt.) microwavable container and micro-cook on HIGH (100%) until melted.
2. Stir in eggs, sugar and vanilla.
3. Blend in flour, baking powder, salt and cocoa.
4. Pour batter into a 2 L (2 qt.) microwavable cake pan. Cover with lid or parchment or wax paper. Micro-cook on MEDIUM (70%) for 6 to 6 $1/2$ minutes or until surface loses its moist appearance. Cool and cut into squares.

1 Serving	Calories	153	Carbohydrate	21 g
	Protein	2 g	Cholesterol	54 mg
	Fat	8 g	Sodium	101 mg

Cereal Bars

16 bars

250 mL	corn syrup	1 cup
75 mL	sugar	$1/3$ cup
250 mL	smooth peanut butter	1 cup
2 L	cereal (Special K, Rice Krispies)	8 cups
125 mL	chocolate chips	$1/2$ cup

1. Combine corn syrup and sugar in a 3 L (3 qt.) microwavable container. Micro-cook on HIGH (100%) for 2 minutes. Stir in peanut butter.
2. Mix quickly with cereal and spread into a oiled 20x20 cm (8x8 inch) square dish. Pack firmly using greased hands. Sprinkle chips on top. Micro-cook on HIGH (100%) for 1 minutes or until chips are soft. Spread to form an icing. Cool and cut into bars.

1 Serving	Calories	225	Carbohydrate	34 g
	Protein	6 g	Cholesterol	0 mg
	Fat	8 g	Sodium	202 mg

For a tasty dessert micro-cook 375 mL (1 $1/2$ cups) chocolate chips on LOW (30%) for 2-3 minutes or just until melted. Watch carefully and stir several times. Combine with 750 mL (3 cups) Rice Krispies. Mold into small custard cups and let cool. Unmould and fill with ice cream. Top with your favorite sauce.

Jam Squares

16 squares

75 mL	butter or margarine	$1/3$ cup
1	egg	1
25 mL	sugar	2 Tbsp.
175 mL	all-purpose flour	$3/4$ cup
2 mL	baking powder	$1/2$ tsp.
125 mL	jam	$1/2$ cup
125 mL	flour	$1/2$ cup
50 mL	butter or margarine	$1/4$ cup
50 mL	brown sugar	$1/4$ cup

1. Combine first amount of butter, egg, sugar, first amount of flour and baking powder, mixing well. Press onto bottom of a 2 L (2 qt.) microwavable cake pan. Cover with lid or parchment or wax paper and micro-cook on MEDIUM (70%) for 3 $1/2$ to 4 minutes or until set and firm.
2. Spread with jam.
3. Combine second amount of flour, second amount of butter and brown sugar until crumbly. Sprinkle over jam. Micro-cook on MEDIUM (70%) for 3 $1/2$ minutes or until jam begins to bubble. Cool before cutting into squares.

1 Serving				
	Calories	155	Carbohydrate	20 g
	Protein	2 g	Cholesterol	30 mg
	Fat	8 g	Sodium	86 mg

Orange Chip Bars

16 bars

375 mL	all-purpose flour	1 ¹/₂ cups
75 mL	powdered milk	¹/₃ cup
75 mL	sugar	¹/₃ cup
5 mL	baking powder	1 tsp.
2 mL	salt	¹/₂ tsp.
125 mL	butter or margarine	¹/₂ cup
125 mL	orange juice	¹/₂ cup
5 mL	vanilla	1 tsp.
5 mL	grated orange rind	1 tsp.
1	egg	1
250 mL	chocolate chips	1 cup

1. Combine dry ingredients. Cut in butter and then stir in orange juice, rind, vanilla and the egg.
2. Stir in the chips and spread in a 2 L (2 qt.) microwavable cake pan. Cover with lid or plastic wrap and micro-cook on MEDIUM (70%) for 6 minutes or until no longer moist on top. Remove cover and let cool before cutting. Spread on glaze if desired.

Glaze:

500 mL	icing sugar	2 cups
5 mL	grated orange rind	1 tsp.
45 mL	orange juice	3 Tbsp.

1. Combine all ingredients.

1 Serving				
	Calories	235	Carbohydrate	37 g
	Protein	3 g	Cholesterol	35 mg
	Fat	9 g	Sodium	150 mg

Shortbread Cookies

24 cookies

175 mL	butter	$3/4$ cup
125 mL	icing sugar	$1/2$ cup
1	egg yolk	1
3 mL	vanilla	$1/2$ tsp.
375 mL	all-purpose flour	$1 1/2$ cups
1 mL	salt	$1/4$ tsp.
1	egg white	1
24	nuts (hazel nuts, whole almonds)	24

1. Cream butter and sugar together very well. Add yolk and vanilla. Blend in flour and salt.
2. Shape into small balls 2.5 cm (1 inch) in diameter. Place 6 at a time on a flat microwavable dish.
3. Beat egg white. Dip a nut into egg white and press into each cookie. Micro-cook on MEDIUM (70%) for 2 to 2 1/2 minutes or until cookies are set. Do not allow to burn. Carefully remove to a cooling rack and repeat until all cookies are baked.

1 Serving	Calories	98	Carbohydrate	9 g
	Protein	1 g	Cholesterol	27 mg
	Fat	6 g	Sodium	74 mg

Caramel Corn

1 L (4 cups)

75 mL	popping corn	$1/3$ cup
45 mL	butter	3 Tbsp.
175 mL	brown sugar	$3/4$ cup
75 mL	peanuts	$1/3$ cup
45 mL	corn syrup	3 Tbsp.
2 mL	vanilla	$1/2$ tsp.
1 mL	baking soda	$1/4$ tsp.
dash	salt	dash

1. Pop corn in a microwavable corn popper, following manufacturer's directions.
2. Place butter in a 3 L (3 qt.) microwavable container. Micro-cook on HIGH (100%) until melted. Stir in sugar, nuts and syrup. Micro-cook on HIGH (100%) for 4 minutes.
3. Add vanilla, salt and soda and mix well. Pour over corn, working quickly and stirring well. Micro-cook on HIGH (100%) for 2 minutes. Stir. Spread out on a buttered surface to cool. Cool 20 to 30 minutes and break apart.

1 serving — 125 mL (½ cup)	Calories	216	Carbohydrate	31 g
	Protein	3 g	Cholesterol	12 mg
	Fat	10 g	Sodium	141 mg

Peanut Brittle

500 g or 1 lb.

250 mL	sugar	1 cup
125 mL	golden corn syrup	1/2 cup
250 mL	roasted, salted peanuts	1 cup
5 mL	butter	1 tsp.
5 mL	vanilla	1 tsp.
5 mL	baking soda	1 tsp.

1. In a 3 L (3 qt.) microwavable container stir together sugar and syrup. Micro-cook on HIGH (100%) for 4 minutes.
2. Stir in peanuts. Micro-cook on HIGH (100%) 3 to 3 1/2 minutes.
3. Add butter and vanilla, blending well. Micro-cook on HIGH (100%) 1 to 1 1/2 minutes. Mixture should be light brown. If not, continue cooking 30 to 60 seconds longer.
4. Add soda and quickly stir until light and foamy. Pour quickly onto greased cookie sheet. Do not spread, but allow mixture to flow. When cool break into pieces.

1 serving — 29 g (1 oz.)	Calories	175	Carbohydrate	25 g
	Protein	4 g	Cholesterol	1 mg
	Fat	8 g	Sodium	160 mg

Candied Pecans

250 mL (1 cup)

A small container filled with these nuts makes an excellent Christmas gift. They taste just like pecan pie.

75 mL	sugar	1/3 cup
25 mL	water	2 Tbsp.
5 mL	cinnamon	1 tsp.
dash	cloves	dash
dash	allspice	dash
2 mL	vanilla	1/2 tsp.
250 mL	pecan halves	1 cup

1. Combine sugar, water and spices in a 750 mL (3 cup) microwavable container. Mix well and micro-cook on HIGH (100%) for 1 1/2 minutes, stirring once. Stir in vanilla.
2. Mix in nuts and micro-cook on HIGH (100%) for 3 to 3 1/2 minutes or until mixture becomes thick and syrupy. Spread on greased foil and break apart with a fork. Cool.

1 serving — 6 pecans	Calories	87	Carbohydrate	10 g
	Protein	1 g	Cholesterol	0 mg
	Fat	5 g	Sodium	1 mg

MISCELLANEOUS

Breads
Dressings
Preserves
Sauces
Cereal

Muffins 'N Marmalade

6-9 muffins

50 mL	butter or margarine	1/4 cup
50 mL	sugar	1/4 cup
50 mL	milk	1/4 cup
1	egg	1
125 mL	all-purpose flour	1/2 cup
75 mL	whole wheat flour	1/3 cup
4 mL	baking powder	3/4 tsp.
1 mL	salt	1/4 tsp.
30 mL	marmalade	2 Tbsp.
15 mL	butter	1 Tbsp.
15 mL	finely chopped walnuts	1 Tbsp.

1. Cream butter and sugar thoroughly. Blend in egg and milk.
2. Combine flours, baking powder and salt. Stir into butter mixture only until just moistened. Place large muffin papers into a microwavable muffin pan. Divide half of batter into the 6 papers. Spoon 5 mL (1 tsp.) of marmalade into centre of each. Top with remaining batter, spreading to cover marmalade. Micro-cook on MEDIUM-LOW (50%) for 5 minutes or until cooked.
3. Melt butter on HIGH (100%) for 30 seconds. Stir in nuts. When muffins are cooked spoon butter mixture over top. Let stand 2 minutes.

1 Serving				
	Calories	164	Carbohydrate	21 g
	Protein	3 g	Cholesterol	52 mg
	Fat	8 g	Sodium	135 mg

◇ *HIGH (100%) power is good for cooking small baked products such as muffins. However, using MEDIUM (70%) will give greater volume.*

Pumpkin Bran Muffins

18 muffins

250 mL	natural bran	1 cup
250 mL	whole wheat flour	1 cup
125 mL	sugar	1/2 cup
7 mL	cinnamon	1 1/2 tsp.
5 mL	baking powder	1 tsp.
5 mL	baking soda	1 tsp.
2 mL	salt	1/2 tsp.
250 mL	pumpkin	1 cup
2	eggs	2
75 mL	oil	1/3 cup
125 mL	milk	1/2 cup
5 mL	lemon juice	1 tsp.
250 mL	raisins	1 cup

1. Combine bran, flour, sugar, cinnamon, baking powder, soda and salt.
2. Combine pumpkin, eggs, oil, milk and lemon juice. Stir into dry ingredients. Blend in raisins.
3. Place large paper liners in vented microwavable muffin cups and fill 2/3 full with batter. Micro-cook 6 at a time on HIGH (100%) for 2 1/2 minutes.

1 Serving				
	Calories	147	Carbohydrate	23 g
	Protein	2 g	Cholesterol	34 mg
	Fat	6 g	Sodium	173 mg

Bacon Cornmeal Muffins

12 muffins

6 slices	bacon	6 slices
50 mL	all-purpose flour	1/4 cup
300 mL	yellow cornmeal	1 1/4 cups
30 mL	sugar	2 Tbsp.
15 mL	baking powder	1 Tbsp.
2 mL	salt	1/2 tsp.
1	egg	1
250 mL	milk	1 cup
	oil	

1. Micro-cook bacon on microwavable bacon rack on HIGH (100%) for 5 to 6 minutes or until crisp. Drain and crumble.
2. Combine flour, cornmeal, sugar, baking powder and salt.
3. Combine egg and milk. Add 45 mL (3 Tbsp.) bacon drippings, using oil if there are not enough drippings. Spoon into large paper liners in a vented microwavable muffin pan. Sprinkle a bit of the crumbled bacon on top of each muffin.
4. Micro-cook on HIGH (100%) for 1 1/2 to 2 1/4 minutes or just until moisture disappears from the surface.

1 Serving	Calories	144	Carbohydrate	18 g
	Protein	4 g	Cholesterol	33 mg
	Fat	6 g	Sodium	173 mg

Sunday Streusel Coffee Cake

Serves 6

Topping:

75 mL	all-purpose flour	1/3 cup
50 mL	butter	1/4 cup
125 mL	brown sugar	1/2 cup
3 mL	cinnamon	1/2 tsp.
125 mL	chopped pecans	1/2 cup

1. Combine all ingredients except pecans and set aside.

Cake:

375 mL	all-purpose flour	1 1/2 cups
10 mL	baking powder	2 tsp.
3 mL	salt	1/2 tsp.
125 mL	sugar	1/2 cup
50 mL	shortening	1/4 cup
1	egg	1
125 mL	milk	1/2 cup

1. Combine flour, baking powder, salt and sugar. Cut in shortening.
2. Combine egg and milk and add to dry mixture, mixing just until combined.
3. Spread in 2 L (2 qt.) thermoplastic cake dish. Spread topping over and sprinkle pecans on top. Cover with parchment or wax paper and micro-cook at MEDIUM (70%) for 5 1/2 to 6 minutes. Let stand 5 minutes before serving.

1 Serving				
	Calories	511	Carbohydrate	71 g
	Protein	7 g	Cholesterol	74 mg
	Fat	23 g	Sodium	277 mg

English Muffin Bread

1 round loaf
(about 40 slices)

English Muffin Bread is almost identical to traditional English Muffins in texture and taste. The only difference is the shape. Delicious served toasted with butter and jam.

75 mL	warm water	¹/₃ cup
15 mL	dry active yeast	1 Tbsp.
10 mL	sugar	2 tsp.
375 mL	milk	1 ¹/₂ cups
7 mL	salt	1 ¹/₂ tsp.
1 mL	baking soda	¹/₄ tsp.
1 L	all-purpose flour	4 cups
	corn meal	

1. Combine water with yeast and sugar and stir until dissolved.
2. Micro-cook milk in a glass measure on HIGH (100%) for
1 minute. Add to yeast mixture. Stir in salt.
3. Place 500 mL (2 cups) flour and soda in a large mixing bowl.
Add yeast mixture and beat well. Add remaining 500 mL (2 cups)
flour and mix well to make a stiff dough.
4. Lightly oil a 3 L (12 cup) thermoplastic tube pan. Sprinkle liberally
with cornmeal. Spoon batter into mould being careful not to disturb
cornmeal coating. Cover and let rise in a warm place until about
2.5 cm (1 inch) below top of dish.
5. Leave covered. Elevate on a microwavable rack and micro-cook
on MEDIUM-LOW (50%) for 7 ¹/₂ minutes or just until top appears
dry. Let stand 10 minutes and turn out onto a rack.
To serve: Slice into thin slices, toast and serve with butter
and jam.

Note: Slice loaf and freeze. Then pop frozen slices into toaster.

1 Serving	Calories	56	Carbohydrate	11 g
	Protein	2 g	Cholesterol	1 mg
	Fat	0 g	Sodium	88 mg

◇ *To speed the rising time of bread, place dough in a microwavable bowl, cover and place in oven. Micro-cook on WARM (10%) for 2 to 5 minutes or just until surface of dough feels slightly warm. Let rest 15 minutes and repeat until dough is doubled in volume. Be sure not to get dough too warm or you will kill the yeast.*

Onion Bread

1 large loaf

1 pkg.	dry onion soup mix	1 pkg.
375 mL	water	1 1/2 cups
15 mL	dry yeast	1 Tbsp.
50 mL	warm water	1/4 cup
30 mL	grated Parmesan cheese	2 Tbsp.
15 mL	sugar	1 Tbsp.
50 mL	oil	1/4 cup
750 mL	all-purpose flour	3 cups

1. Combine soup mix and first amount of water in a 2 L (2 qt.) microwavable container. Micro-cook on HIGH (100%) for 5 minutes. Cool to lukewarm.
2. Soften yeast in 50 mL (1/4 cup) warm water.
3. Add cheese, sugar and oil to onion mixture. Stir in 250 mL (1 cup) flour and blend in well. Add yeast mixture. Add enough remaining flour to make a stiff dough. Turn out on floured surface and knead until smooth.
4. Lightly grease a 2 L(2 qt.) microwavable bowl. Place dough in bowl turning to grease surface. Cover and let rise in a warm place until double, about 45 minutes to 1 hour.
5. Remove cover and micro-cook on MEDIUM (70%) for 7 minutes or until cooked. Allow to stand 5 minutes and remove from bowl.

1 Serving					
	Calories	54	Carbohydrate	8 g	
	Protein	1 g	Cholesterol	0 mg	
	Fat	2 g	Sodium	30 mg	

Bacon Dressing

Makes 175 mL (¾ cup)

Delicious served over a salad of assorted greens.

3 slices	bacon	3 slices
125 mL	light cream	½ cup
2	egg yolks	2
dash	salt and pepper	dash
50 mL	wine vinegar	¼ cup
10 mL	sugar	2 tsp.

1. Cut bacon into cubes and micro-cook in a 750 mL (3 cup) microwavable container until crisp. Remove bacon. Allow grease to cool slightly.
2. Blend yolks and cream into grease. Add salt, pepper, vinegar and sugar. Micro-cook at LOW (30%) until thickened, stirring 2 to 3 times. Do not overcook or it will curdle.
3. Sprinkle bacon over greens and toss with dressing.

1 Serving — 15 mL (1 Tbsp.)	Calories	64	Carbohydrate	1 g
	Protein	1 g	Cholesterol	55 mg
	Fat	6 g	Sodium	62 mg

Cooked Salad Dressing

Makes 250 mL (1 cup)

When fresh tomatoes are in season keep this on hand for a delicious salad.

15 mL	cornstarch	1 Tbsp.
75 mL	sugar	⅓ cup
5 mL	dry mustard	1 tsp.
1 mL	salt	¼ tsp.
50 mL	milk	¼ cup
1	egg	1
75 mL	cider vinegar	⅓ cup

1. Combine cornstarch, sugar, dry mustard and salt in a 750 mL (3 cup) microwavable container. Blend in milk. Micro-cook on HIGH (100%) until thickened and bubbly, about 1 ½ minutes. Stir twice.
2. Whisk egg and slowly pour cornstarch mixture in. Blend well. Stir in vinegar and micro-cook on MEDIUM (70%) 1 to 1 ¼ minutes or until thickened. Stir several times during cooking.
Store covered in refrigerator.

1 Serving — 15 mL (1 Tbsp.)	Calories	31	Carbohydrate	6 g
	Protein	1 g	Cholesterol	19 mg
	Fat	1 g	Sodium	37 mg

Red Pepper Relish

6 jars (125 mL or 4 oz.)

This relish is excellent as an appetizer: Spread melba toast rounds or crackers with cream cheese and top with a bit of relish. Make double quantities to use for gifts.

250 mL	sweet red pepper, finely chopped	1 cup
750 mL	sugar	3 cups
175 mL	cider vinegar	3/4 cup
1/2 bottle	Certo	1/2 bottle

1. Place peppers in a 3 L (3 qt.) microwavable container. Add sugar and vinegar. Micro-cook on HIGH (100%) approximately 8 minutes or until mixture comes to a full boil. Stir every three minutes. Once the mixture is boiling continue to micro-cook on HIGH (100%) for 1 minute longer.
2. Stir in Certo and stir mixture for 5 to 10 minutes. Pour into sterilized jars. Seal with 1/4 inch melted paraffin.

1 serving — 15 mL (1 Tbsp.)	Calories	45	Carbohydrate	12 g
	Protein	0 g	Cholesterol	0 mg
	Fat	0 g	Sodium	0 mg

◇ *Paraffin will not melt in the microwave oven because it does not absorb microwave energy. To melt paraffin, place it in a small microwavable container and set the container in a larger microwavable container filled half full with hot water. Micro-cook on MEDIUM (70%) until paraffin is melted.*

◇ *To sterilize jars for jam or relish, fill almost full with hot water and place in oven. Micro-cook on HIGH (100%) until water is boiling. Let water stand in jars until ready to fill.*

Bacon Melts
Bacon Sticks
Cocktail Almonds
Crackers and Cream Cheese
with Red Pepper Relish

Strawberry Jam

1.25 L (5 cups)

2 L	**fresh strawberries**	**2 qt.**
45 mL	**Certo crystals ($^1/_2$ box)**	**3 Tbsp.**
750 mL	**sugar**	**3 cups**

1. Wash and hull strawberries. Mash or crush and then measure. There should be 500 mL (2 cups).
2. Combine berries and Certo in a 3 L (3 qt.) microwavable container. Micro-cook on HIGH (100%) for 5 to 6 minutes or until jam comes to a boil, stirring once.
3. Add sugar and mix well. Micro-cook on HIGH (100%) for 4 to 5 minutes or until jam has come to a full rolling boil. Continue to cook for 1 full minute, stirring once.
4. Stir jam and skim foam from top. Let cool for 5 minutes and ladle into sterilized jars. Seal with paraffin or a canning lid.

1 serving — 15 mL (1 Tbsp.)	Calories	39	Carbohydrate	10 g
	Protein	0 g	Cholesterol	0 mg
	Fat	0 g	Sodium	0 mg

Hollandaise Sauce

Makes 250 mL (1 cup)

45 mL	freshly squeezed lemon juice	3 Tbsp.
2 mL	dry mustard	1/2 tsp.
2	egg yolks	2
1 mL	salt	1/4 tsp.
dash	white pepper	dash
125 mL	butter	1/2 cup

1. Mix lemon juice with mustard, egg yolks, salt and pepper.
2. Place butter in a 750 mL (3 cup) microwavable container.
Micro-cook on HIGH (100%) for 1 minute.
3. Whisk egg yolk mixture into hot butter, blending well. Micro-cook on MEDIUM (70%) for 1 minute or until sauce thickens, stirring every 20 seconds. BE SURE SAUCE DOES NOT BOIL.

1 Serving — 15 mL (1 Tbsp.)	Calories	63	Carbohydrate	0 g
	Protein	0 g	Cholesterol	50 mg
	Fat	7 g	Sodium	93 mg

BEARNAISE SAUCE:
Use 25 mL (2 Tbsp.) white wine in place of 25 mL (2 Tbsp.) lemon juice and add 1 finely chopped green onion at end.

Basic White Sauce

Makes 125 mL (1/2 cup)

15 mL	butter	1 Tbsp.
15 mL	all-purpose flour	1 Tbsp.
1 mL	salt	1/4 tsp.
dash	pepper	dash
125 mL	milk	1/2 cup

1. In a 750 mL (3 cup) microwavable container micro-cook butter on HIGH (100%) until melted. Blend in flour and salt.
2. Micro-cook milk on HIGH (100%) for 1 minute or until hot but not boiling. Blend milk into flour mixture and micro-cook on HIGH (100%) until boiling, stirring every 30 seconds.

1 Serving — 15 mL (1 Tbsp.)	Calories	25	Carbohydrate	2 g
	Protein	1 g	Cholesterol	5 mg
	Fat	2 g	Sodium	82 mg

CHEESE SAUCE:
When sauce is cooked, stir in 50 mL (1/4 cup) grated cheese (Cheddar, Swiss, Colby) and let stand 1 minute.

Grand Marnier Sauce For Fruit

Makes 250 mL (1 cup)

125 mL	milk	1/2 cup
30 mL	sugar	2 Tbsp.
3 mL	cornstarch	1/2 tsp.
1	egg yolk	1
30 mL	Grand Marnier or other orange liqueur	2 Tbsp.
1	egg white	1

1. In a 750 mL (3 cup) microwavable container combine milk, sugar and cornstarch. Micro-cook on HIGH (100%) for 1 to 2 minutes or until thickened and boiling, stirring several times.
2. Beat egg yolk and gradually stir in hot sauce. Blend well. Micro-cook on MEDIUM (50%) for 30 seconds or until thickened and smooth, being careful not to boil.
3. Blend in Grand Marnier. Beat egg white until stiff and blend in.

1 Serving — 15 mL (1 Tbsp.)	Calories	20	Carbohydrate	3 g
	Protein	1 g	Cholesterol	18 mg
	Fat	0 g	Sodium	7 mg

Custard Sauce

Makes 300 mL (1 1/4 cups)

250 mL	milk	1 cup
2	eggs	2
50 mL	sugar	1/4 cup
2 mL	vanilla	1/2 tsp.

1. Micro-cook milk in a 750 mL (3 cup) microwavable container on HIGH (100%) for 2 minutes or until hot but not boiling.
2. Blend eggs and sugar and whisk into milk. Micro-cook on MEDIUM (70%) for 2 1/2 minutes, stirring every 30 seconds or until thickened. Do not allow to boil. Stir in vanilla.

1 Serving — 15 mL (1 Tbsp.)	Calories	22	Carbohydrate	3 g
	Protein	1 g	Cholesterol	26 mg
	Fat	1 g	Sodium	11 mg

Sweet and Sour Sauce

Makes 500 mL (2 cups)

This is enough for 1 pound (500g) fish or meatballs or chicken pieces.

1 can(540mL)	pineapple tidbits	1 can(19 oz.)
15 mL	cornstarch	1 Tbsp.
50 mL	sugar	¼ cup
25 mL	cider vinegar	2 Tbsp.
15 mL	soy sauce	1 Tbsp.
1	small green pepper	1
25 mL	ketchup	2 Tbsp.
dash	ginger	dash

1. Drain juice from pineapple and add water to make 250 mL (1 cup).
2. In a 750 mL (3 cup) microwavable container combine cornstarch and sugar. Stir in juice and micro-cook on HIGH (100%) until mixture boils, stirring just before it comes to a boil. Stir and bring to a boil again, about 3 to 4 minutes.
3. Cut green pepper into squares and add to sauce with remaining ingredients. Micro-cook on HIGH (100%) for 2 to 3 minutes or until green pepper is slightly soft. Stir in pineapple chunks.

1 Serving — 50 mL (¼ cup)				
	Calories	84	Carbohydrate	22 g
	Protein	0 g	Cholesterol	0 mg
	Fat	0 g	Sodium	45 mg

Barbecue Sauce

Makes about 500 mL (2 cups)

Make this and keep in refrigerator for use when barbecuing chicken or pork chops, or serve over meatballs or fish.

250 mL	ketchup	1 cup
125 mL	water	1/2 cup
10 mL	dry mustard	2 tsp.
10 mL	brown sugar	2 tsp.
5 mL	onion powder	1 tsp.
50 mL	red wine vinegar	1/4 cup
30 mL	Worcestershire sauce	2 Tbsp.
10 mL	chili powder	2 tsp.
5 mL	salt	1 tsp.
dash	pepper	dash
5 mL	oregano	1 tsp.
1	bay leaf	1
1 clove	garlic, minced	1 clove

1. Combine all ingredients in a 4 L (4 cup) microwavable container and micro-cook on HIGH (100%) about 5 minutes or until sauce begins to bubble. Reduce power to LOW (30%) and micro-cook 5 minutes longer.
2. Store in a glass container in the refrigerator.

1 Serving — 15 mL (1 Tbsp.)				
Calories	13	Carbohydrate	3 g
Protein	57 g	Cholesterol	0 mg
Fat	0 g	Sodium	158 mg

All-Purpose Tomato Sauce

Makes 1.25 L (5 cups)

This freezes well and is nice to serve over chicken or meat loaf.
Perfect for spaghetti.

1	green pepper, chopped	1
3-4	large onions	3-4
75 mL	oil	$1/3$ cup
2 cans(798mL)	canned tomatoes	2 cans(28 oz.)
1 can(398 mL)	tomato paste	1 can(14 oz.)
10 mL	beef soup base	2 tsp.
15 mL	Worcestershire sauce	1 Tbsp.
15 mL	basil or oregano	1 Tbsp.
15 mL	dried parsley	1 Tbsp.
2 mL	salt	$1/2$ tsp.
1 mL	pepper	$1/4$ tsp.
2	bay leaves	2

1. Micro-cook green pepper, onion and oil in a 3 L (3 qt.) microwavable container on HIGH (100%) for 5 to 6 minutes.
2. Add remaining ingredients. Cover and micro-cook on HIGH (100%) for 10 to 12 minutes. Stir and micro-cook on MEDIUM-LOW (50%) for 60 minutes, stirring every 15 minutes.

1 Serving — 125 mL (½ cup)	Calories	142	Carbohydrate	16 g
	Protein	3 g	Cholesterol	0 mg
	Fat	8 g	Sodium	531 mg

Breakfast Cereal

Serves 2

50 mL	Oat Bran cereal	1/4 cup
50 mL	Cream of Wheat	1/4 cup
2 mL	cinnamon	1/2 tsp.
50 mL	raisins	1/4 cup
0.5 mL	salt	1/8 tsp.
15 mL	brown sugar	1 Tbsp.
300 mL	hot water	1 1/4 cups

1. Combine all ingredients in a 1 L (4 cup) microwavable container. Micro-cook on HIGH (100%) for 3 minutes or until cereal is thickened and comes to a boil. Stir after 2 minutes. Serve with milk and brown sugar.

1 serving	Calories	190	Carbohydrate	44 g
	Protein	4 g	Cholesterol	0 mg
	Fat	2 g	Sodium	54 mg

Cinnamon Apple Oatmeal

Serves 1

50 mL	oatmeal	1/4 cup
175 mL	water	3/4 cup
1/4	apple, peeled, cored and chopped	1/4
dash	cinnamon	dash

1. Combine all ingredients in a 750 mL (3 cup) microwavable container. Micro-cook on HIGH (100%) for 2 minutes or until cereal is cooked. Let stand 2 minutes.
2. Serve with milk and brown sugar.

1 serving	Calories	102	Carbohydrate	20 g
	Protein	3 g	Cholesterol	0 mg
	Fat	2 g	Sodium	1 mg

Granola

1.25L (5 cups)

875 mL	large flake oatmeal	3 ½ cups
2 mL	salt	½ tsp.
125 mL	coconut	½ cup
125 mL	wheat germ	½ cup
125 mL	chopped almonds	½ cup
50 mL	brown sugar	¼ cup
50 mL	oil	¼ cup
50 mL	honey	¼ cup

1. Combine oatmeal, salt, coconut, wheat germ, almonds and sugar, blending well.
2. Combine oil and honey. Stir into oatmeal mixture and mix thoroughly.
3. Pour into a 2 L (2 qt.) microwavable cake pan and micro-cook on HIGH (100%) for 7 to 9 minutes or until nicely browned, stirring every 2 minutes. Stir mixture several times as it cools. Store in an air-tight container.

1 serving — 125 mL (½ cup)	Calories	268	Carbohydrate	33 g
	Protein	6 g	Cholesterol	0 mg
	Fat	13 g	Sodium	100 mg

◇ *If honey becomes crystalline, micro-cook on LOW (30%) for 1 to 2 minutes, stirring frequently, until it becomes liquid again. Be careful not to get it too hot.*

Index

198

Please send _____ copies of **Meals Microwave Style** at $14.99 per copy plus $2.00 each for handling.

Name: _____

Address: _____

_____

Postal Code: _____

Enclosed is $ _____

Make cheque or money order payable to:

Gai-Garet Design & Publication Ltd.
P.O. Box 424
Carp, Ontario, Canada
K0A 1L0

- -

Please send _____ copies of **Meals Microwave Style** at $14.99 per copy plus $2.00 each for handling.

Name: _____

Address: _____

_____

Postal Code: _____

Enclosed is $ _____

Make cheque or money order payable to:

Gai-Garet Design & Publication Ltd.
P.O. Box 424
Carp, Ontario, Canada
K0A 1L0